Transition Teaming:
26 Strategies
for Interagency Collaboration

Pattie Noonan

Council for
Exceptional
Children

A publication of the Division on Career Development and Transition of the Council for Exceptional Children

Strategy 11 is adapted with permission from the *Arizona Community Transition Teams Training Manual and the Kansas Transition Council Workbook*, by M. Morningstar, P. Noonan, and J. Soukup. Copyright 2010 University of Kansas Center for Research on Learning. Activity 12.1 is adapted with permission from *Essential Tools*, by R. A. Stodden, S. E. Brown, L. M. Galloway, S. Mrazek, and L. Noy. Copyright 2005 National Center on Secondary Education and Transition.

© 2014 by Council for Exceptional Children
2900 Crystal Drive, Suite 1000
Arlington, Virginia 22202-3557
www.cec.sped.org

Library of Congress Cataloging-in-Publication data
Noonan, Pattie.
Transition Teaming: 26 Strategies for Interagency Collaboration by Pattie Noonan.
p. cm.
Includes biographical references.

ISBN 978-0-86586-477-1

Book design and layout by Carol L. Williams

Printed in the United States of America
10 9 8 7 6 5 4 3 2 1

Stock No. P6119

Contents

Foreword by Gary M. Clark   v

Acknowledgments   vii

Chapter 1   Introduction 1

Chapter 2   Building Collaborative Skills 7
With Amy Gaumer Erickson

     Strategy 1:   Gain an Understanding of How Co-Workers' Jobs Are Related to Transition

     Strategy 2:   Increase Awareness and Knowledge of Adult Agency Services

     Strategy 3:   Gain Administrator Buy-in

     Strategy 4:   Communicate Information About Transition to Co-Workers

     Strategy 5:   Communicate Information About Transition to the Local Community

     Strategy 6:   Communicate Information About Transition to Families

     Strategy 7:   Coordinate With Co-Workers to Provide Transition Services

     Strategy 8:   Coordinate With Agency Representatives to Provide Transition Services

     Strategy 9:   Participate in Professional Development Related to Transition

     Strategy 10:   Participate in Professional Development Sponsored by Community Agencies

Chapter 3   Forming a Community Transition Team 45
With Jennifer Brussow

     Strategy 11:   Develop a Community Transition Team

     Strategy 12:   Identify a Shared Vision

Strategy 13: Conduct Effective Community Transition
Team Meetings
Strategy 14: Organize Your Community Transition Team
Strategy 15: Map Community Resources
Strategy 16: Enlist Community Members for Help

Chapter 4   Becoming a High-Functioning Community Transition Team 71

Strategy 17: Build Team Structure
Strategy 18: Develop Action-Oriented Teaming
Strategy 19: Come to Consensus
Strategy 20: Assess Shared Leadership

Chapter 5   Using Data to Inform Decision Making 91
With Madeline Wetta

Strategy 21: Use Data as a Community Transition Team
Strategy 22: Use Data Already Available to Your
Community Transition Team
Strategy 23: Gather Information and Collect Data

Chapter 6   Sustaining Collaborative Efforts 109
Strategy 24: Plan for Sustainability
Strategy 25: Develop Bylaws
Strategy 26: Develop a Memorandum of Understanding

Appendix 125
Tool #1:   Transition Collaboration Strategies Strengths and Weaknesses
Tool #2:   Teaching Practices Supporting College and Career Readiness
Tool #3:   Transition Assessment Framework
Tool #4:   Meeting Agenda
Tool #5:   Process Checklist
Tool #6:   Team Functioning Scale
Tool #7:   Action Plan Template
Tool #8:   Shared Leadership Survey
Tool #9:   Sustainability Survey and Sustained Teaming Activities Checklist
Tool #10:   Sample Bylaws

References   147

Foreword

Experienced gardeners often say that for many plants (hosta in particular), there are three stages of growth and maturity: first year sleep, second year creep, and third year leap. This is a metaphor for human services. Progress is slow and variable, as with any systemic change. Like plants, human services need nurturing and continuing care. Agencies and institutions are subject to politics, policies and priorities (freezes, droughts, floods), nay sayers and ax grinders (pests), loss of interest or energy (aging, fad followers, or fair-weather workers), and the continuous cycles of change in personnel who work in the field.

One of the pleasures of working in a complex area of human services for over 50 years is seeing progress over time. We can see this in education, civil rights, science and technology, medical and health practices, and social services. None of the advances made in these fields have come quickly, or without trial and error, surges of progress, and slides into complacency and mediocrity. Because human services for the vast majority of the general public are largely dependent upon government (federal, state, and local) or quasi-government agencies, human services professionals often have to ride the waves of new initiatives, minimal funding, funding cuts, changes in priorities for service priorities, and the vagaries of political debates and compromise (or lack of compromise).

We have made slow but steady progress in providing transition services, not only in the number of individuals and their families who receive services, but also in the quality and variety of services that they receive. This progress has been more rapid and impressive in some states than others and more effective in some school districts than others, even within the same states. In my opinion, what contributes most to the success of those states or school districts is captured in this book. The creativity, wisdom, and commitment of scattered professionals in forging partnerships through cooperation, coordination, coalition, and collaboration come out in page after page of this book. I am delighted to see after all these years a sharing of current strategies that can work for collaborative efforts between schools and state and community human service agencies.

Do a quick scan to see what is available to you in this book. Dive into chapters or specific strategies that you need to know how to do, or do better right now. Read it from cover to cover. Whatever your style, keep this book in your professional library as a treasure of practical information and an ever-ready handbook for your opportunities and challenges in collaboration.

Gary M. Clark, Ed.D.
Professor Emeritus
University of Kansas

Acknowledgments

First and foremost, I would like to thank the educators, administrators, families, professionals, and students with whom I have had the pleasure to work over the past decade. Their commitment to quality transition education and services to promote positive postschool outcomes continues to impress and inspire. Day after day, secondary special educators go above and beyond their job descriptions to provide quality experiences for youth and young adults with (and without) disabilities through their personal dedication, pursuit of continuous improvement, and unflinching faith in the capacity of our students.

This book would not have been possible without the help and contributions of dedicated colleagues and staff. Dr. Amy Gaumer Erickson's partnership and friendship have informed and shaped these strategies throughout our ongoing collaboration. Dr. Jane Soukup and Linda Cantrell have contributed years of hard work overcoming challenges to collaboration through teaming, problem solving, and complex thinking in support of teachers. Jennifer Brussow and Madeline Wetta spent significant time assisting with the development of this book. It would be tough to find a better team. I would also like to thank Drs. Mary Morningstar, Gary Clark, and Jim Martin for their continual guidance and support over the years, as well as the Council for Exceptional Children (CEC) and its Division on Career Development and Transition (DCDT) for their work in supporting teachers and promoting high-quality adult outcomes for people with disabilities.

Strategies in this book originated from research and projects conducted in multiple states (special thanks to the Missouri Department of Elementary and Secondary Education, Arizona Department of Education Exceptional Student Services, and the Kansas and Oregon Departments of Education). I also would like to thank the educators, school districts, and community transition teams who have so graciously allowed me to include their work as examples. In addition, I am grateful to the state professionals and community transition teams all over the country who work to promote collaboration, including people like Barb Gilpin and Pam Williams, Lorrie Sheehy and Alissa Trollinger, Ranita Wilks and Kerry Haag (KS), Martha Buenrostro (OR), and Sarah Stone; school districts such as Tigard Tualatin, Colorado River Union, Gasconade County R-1, Kirksville, Ft. Osage, St. Louis Special, Tucson Unified, Fredericktown, Show Low, Flowing Wells, West Plains, and Phoenix Union High; and teams, organizations, and agencies such as Seneca Community Transition Team, Missouri Interagency State Transition Team, the Office of the State Superintendent of Education, Columbia Community Transition Team, the Louisiana Employment Empowerment Program, Grain Valley Empower Community Transition Team, Mountain View-Birch Tree Life Changing Network Community Transition Team, Northwest Community Transition Team, Westside-Exit Connections Community Transition Team, Branson Community Transition Team, A Cup on the Hill, Engage Community Transition Team, Endless Possibilities Community Transition Team, and H.I.T. Team (Scott County R-IV).

I'd also like to thank my parents for maintaining high expectations, even during challenging times, and instilling me with the confidence to support teachers.

Finally, the strategies in this book represent hours on the road away from my supportive husband, John Green. Much, if not all, of this book is due to his ongoing support, listening skills, and ability to hold down the fort.

My experiences as a teacher, professional development provider, researcher, and evaluator have convinced me of the value of collaboration. However, I have also learned that people need strategies in order to collaborate effectively; thus, I envisioned a book that would gather those resources and strategies. This book is the realization of that vision: a collection of collaborative strategies that have worked for teachers and community transition teams.

Thank you all for your help.

P. N.

Chapter 1

Introduction

Collaboration and transition education and services have gone hand in hand since the creation of secondary special education. Because the field of transition envisions a seamless movement between our education system and real-world employment, it in effect is charging educators, adult services professionals, colleges, and employers to work more closely together to ensure high-quality adult living for people with disabilities.

As we all know, adolescents with disabilities making the transition from school to adult life need lots of support, especially when it comes to finding and sustaining employment, living independently, and pursuing postsecondary education and training. Many students will be involved with a wide range of community services both before and after graduation. Whereas some services may be time-limited (e.g., vocational rehabilitation, VR), many are ongoing supports (e.g., mental health services, in-home support services).

Although we all agree that we need to work together to serve students, outcomes for youths with disabilities remain poor, and youths with disabilities are not achieving outcomes comparable to their typically developing peers (D. R. Johnson, Thurlow, & Stout, 2007; Newman, Wagner, Cameto, Knokey, & Shaver, 2010; Taylor, Krane, & Orkis, 2010). In general, they are more likely to drop out of high school, remain unemployed or underemployed, receive federal assistance, not attend postsecondary education (or fail in the first year), and suffer from health issues (Freudenberg & Ruglis, 2007; Hair, Ling, & Cochran, 2003; National High School Center, 2007; Swanson, 2009). Schools, it seems, often fail to create linkages and provide coordinated services promoting postschool success.

Consider the image of the crew building the train track and the caption "Team Work." Humorous cartoons depicting teamwork (see Figure 1.1) resonate as all too familiar to educators and adult agency staff. Many if not all of us have participated in nonfunctioning groups or teams that have lost sight of their true goals (e.g., high-quality adult outcomes for youth with disabilities). Too often, personalities and turf wars, lack of administrative support, and barriers such as lack of time and communication contribute to poor planning and implementation of key services.

Because of the complex needs of our students, schools cannot be the sole provider of transition services. Schools and community agencies must work together to provide transition services for youth with disabilities. Effective transition requires the resources and expertise of adult service agencies, community groups, employers, and professional disciplines. Because adult and community services are based upon eligibility, it's essential for agencies to be part of the transition process as early as possible (Cozzens, Dowdy, & Smith, 1999; Hasazi, Furney, DeStefano, & Johnson, 1999; L. J. Johnson, Zorn, Tam, Lamontagne, & Johnson, 2003; Noyes & Sax, 2004).

Figure 1.1
Team Work

Note. Reprinted with permission from Ahajokes.

What Is Collaboration?

Collaboration is mentioned regularly in our work, but rarely defined. Meetings are scheduled to encourage "collaboration," but attendees may be unclear of the purpose or end goal. This book will illustrate that collaboration is not a one-time event, but instead a developmental process that involves multiple agencies working together in business, health, social services, and education partnerships (L. J. Johnson et al., 2003). Each agency participates within its own system and at its own pace, continually developing toward the goal of providing better services in collaboration with others (Kleinhammer-Tramill & Rosenkoetter, 1994; Timmons, Cohen, & Fesko, 2004).

To put it simply, collaboration is "a way of thinking and relating, a philosophy, a paradigm shift, an attitude change. It requires a set of behaviors, beliefs, attitudes, and values. The result is a sense of shared ownership, shared responsibility, and shared success" (Bishop, Wolf, & Arango, 1993, pp. 11–12). Imagine a line of four construction workers carrying a large beam across a gap. As each construction worker crosses the gap, the three others work together to support the weight of the person over the gap. As the whole group crosses, each person is supported by the others in turn. All four workers share a common goal as well as a mutually beneficial relationship. This level of support is necessary to deliver the beam to the other side of the gap. They work together to support each other, with each worker carrying a larger load at times in order to achieve the end goal.

This same concept can be applied to collaboration in transition, as individuals work toward a shared vision of quality adult outcomes for youth. Various entities such as educators, vocational rehabilitation, and one-stop centers can collaborate first by building relationships and determining a shared vision. Next, individuals need to identify mutual goals (e.g., increased employment opportunities for young adults) and determine each member's responsibilities for activities to meet the goals. Finally, team members share resources, knowledge, and expertise as well as the rewards from successful outcomes (Mattessich, 2003; PACER Center, n.d.). If these steps don't fall into place immediately, don't despair; the road to interagency collaboration is not an easy one. You may encounter several advances and setbacks before achieving strong collaborative relationships.

Collaboration does not happen overnight. Research has determined that relationships progress through distinct stages on the way to collaboration (deFur, 1997; Dunst & Bruder, 2002; Frey, Lohmeier, Lee, Tollefson, & Johanning, 2006; Gajda, 2004; Hogue, 1993; Peterson, 1991). As educators and adult agency staff begin to collaborate, it is helpful to understand that there are five stages of interagency collaboration: networking, cooperation, coordination, coalition, and collaboration (Frey et al., 2006). Before collaboration begins, the two entities have no interaction at all, and they can be said to exist at a "zero" level of collaboration.

The first stage of collaborative relationships, networking, occurs as team members discover a wide range of services available in their community and are able to make referrals to other agencies. Networking is characterized by low levels of cooperation, with agencies and educators communicating for the purposes of referral only (Cashman, 1995). An example would be an educator providing transitioning students with a set of pamphlets on local housing programs.

The second stage, cooperation, involves two-way communication between parties and somewhat defined collaborative roles. However, in this stage, agencies and educators continue to practice independent decision making and formal communication. For example, if an educator and an adult service agency discuss a need for summer work experiences, but continue to make decisions about the issue independently with limited communication, they are exhibiting cooperation.

Coordination, the third stage, is an ongoing process that involves sharing information and resources, establishing defined roles, and communicating frequently. Some shared decision making also occurs in this stage. When engaging in coordination with other agencies, you must continually seek the services, supports, and resources necessary to benefit each student's changing situation (Dunst & Bruder, 2002). Service coordination assures that services will be provided in an integrated and coordinated way.

A transition services practitioner who refers a student for VR services, invites the VR counselor to the student's annual individualized education program (IEP) meeting, and maintains ongoing contact with the VR counselor is exhibiting coordination.

4

Coalition, the fourth stage of interagency collaboration, requires interaction and agreement. It is characterized by shared decision-making responsibilities, accountability, and trust. This stage requires high levels of input and commitment from each participant. Where cooperation exists, agencies begin to jointly schedule activities and planning times and work as a team (Cashman, 1995; deFur, 1997). One example is a community transition council composed of local education agency representatives and various adult service organizations. The transition council's mission is to align programming and services to best meet the needs of local youth with disabilities; in order to accomplish this mission, all participants must work together to schedule events and conduct outreach.

5

The fifth and highest stage is collaboration, which can be defined as a process through which parties with different perspectives explore their differences and search for innovative solutions (Cashman, 1995; deFur, 1997). When agencies collaborate, they work within one shared system to solve problems, share decision-making responsibilities, and merge resources. Members of a collaborative transition team make better decisions as a group, as their collective wisdom provides multiple options and helps to overcome barriers. An example of high levels of collaboration would be the formation of a community-based program for 18- to 21-year-olds in which half the services are funded through the local school and half are funded by an adult services agency. For this program, staffing and daily programming would be coordinated and shared for all students. Although not all problems require this level of collaboration and there is value in each level, full collaboration is necessary for many of the complex issues educators face.

Interagency collaboration promotes the most efficient service delivery systems while also reducing operational costs, as specialized agencies and disciplines can work together to fill gaps in service systems (L. J. Johnson et al., 2003). But, most important, interagency collaboration can provide a support network to ensure that individuals can participate and achieve the outcomes they choose (Morningstar, Kleinhammer-Tramill, & Lattin, 1999). By advancing through the stages of collaboration, educators, adult services staff, employers, and families can develop skills to move beyond merely making referrals and instead become partners with shared goals and successes (Cashman, 1995; deFur, 1997; Dunst & Bruder, 2002).

What Does This Mean to Me? Understanding Changing Roles in Interagency Collaboration

Although we likely agree that interagency collaboration is important, many secondary special educators are unprepared for this daunting task. Many teachers receive limited or no preservice education in how to network, coordinate services, or even reach out to other stakeholders for collaborative efforts. In fact, these activities may seem foreign when compared to the traditional approach to secondary special education. Despite the fact that teachers receive limited preparation or training in this area, we need to work with other entities to promote and ensure successful postschool outcomes for our students. Often, this requires that we shift our role to include coordinating services with other providers to meet the diverse needs of students.

A specialized skill set is required for educators who provide transition services as they work to coordinate services with adult agency representatives to meet the individualized needs of students. Asselin, Todd-Allen, & deFur (1998) identified facilitating intraschool and interagency linkages as critical duties of the educator who provides transition services. Providers of transition education and services must have knowledge of agencies and have high levels of interpersonal communication skills to work well with others (deFur & Taymans, 1995).

In 2000, the Division on Career Development and Transition (DCDT), a division of the Council for Exceptional Children, defined an educator who provides transition services as "an individual who plans, coordinates, delivers, and evaluates transition education and services at the school or system level, in conjunction with other educators, families, students, and representatives of community organizations" (p. 1). One of the identified competencies for transition specialists, "Communication and Collaborative Partnerships," focuses on having the knowledge and skills to work with both adult agencies and families (DCDT, 2000). Interagency collaboration is a key component of transition and a critical skill area for transition specialists. The ability to build relationships is a gateway to gaining the knowledge and skills needed to develop collaborative partnerships.

Interagency collaboration in transition should be purposeful and systematic. We know that deliberate actions on the part of professionals can promote interagency collaboration. Effective interagency collaboration often requires a change in participants' behavior. Team members must pay increased attention to both the process of collaboration and its goal while maintaining a student-centered focus (Cashman, 1995; deFur, 1997). Collaborative planning and service delivery require a team whose members understand complex service issues and have the skills and willingness to work with others (deFur, 1997; Mattessich & Monsey, 1992). Collaborative planning can be accomplished through strategies such as cross training and frequent meetings to increase communication (Timmons et al., 2004). The end result will be high levels of trust and a sense of mutual responsibility.

What Is the Vision of This Book?

The overall vision of this book is to give providers of secondary special education concrete strategies for building collaborative relationships. The book is structured by topic, so readers can consume the material front-to-back or peruse strategies based on their immediate needs.

Chapter 2 describes various strategies that individual educators can use on their own to improve their collaboration immediately. Through reflection, increased awareness of partners, relationship-building activities, and outreach, educators can expand their collaboration on a personal level, thus paving the way for more fruitful group collaboration.

Once you have expanded your individual capacity for collaboration, Chapter 3 provides ways to expand the focus of your collaborative activities by forming a community transition team. Community transition teams are teams of educators, families, adult agencies, and employers with the mission of enabling students with disabilities to achieve their goals and dreams for the future. Creating a community transition team will help increase the levels of collaboration between parties and enable targeted action to support students with disabilities.

Chapter 4 suggests strategies to increase the levels of collaboration so that you have a high-functioning community transition team. These activities will help you structure, organize, and manage your team for maximum effectiveness.

As your community transition team continues its work, it's important to make sure your decisions and future directions are based on data from your school district, region, and state. Chapter 5 covers the collection and use of data on postschool outcomes, academic achievement, student behavior and school discipline, and local and regional employment trends. In addition, this chapter explains how your team may find it beneficial to collect data on your community in order to tailor your goals to your unique situation.

Once your team is established, functioning effectively, and making decisions based on the appropriate data, you may think your work is over. However, all transition teams will encounter new challenges as circumstances, agencies, and members change. Chapter 6 covers sustainability for your community team by addressing common obstacles, helping you develop agreements to plan for future changes, and providing a sustainability survey to allow you to anticipate challenges and plan for the future.

The Appendix provides blank versions of the surveys and tools discussed throughout the book. These process tools can be copied and used throughout your journey of creating and sustaining your community transition team. The Appendix also includes guidelines for administration, interpretation, and application to help you use these measures successfully.

Finally, it is important to acknowledge that as you charge yourself to collaborate more individually and through teaming structures, you will encounter barriers along with way (e.g., lack of time, lack of administrative support, fatigue). Take heart, as this is a normal part of change. Throughout the book, "Roadblock Alert!" sections are interspersed to help you problem-solve barriers as they arise and proceed with working together to maximize impact.

Chapter 2

Building Collaborative Skills

With Amy Gaumer Erickson

The goal of this chapter is to provide concrete strategies that you can implement on your own to improve collaboration both with colleagues in your school and with professionals in your community. Although comprehensive changes for the youth in your community often requires a team approach (addressed in Chapters 3–5), expanded collaboration through building collaborative relationships only requires willingness on your part. Of course, time is required as well; the strategies discussed in this chapter are designed to be implemented without an extensive time commitment. Often, these strategies can be embedded into your job to improve transition outcomes for students in your community. This chapter provides activities that you can start implementing, today.

Collaboration must begin with building collaborative, trusting relationships. One educator who provides transition services commented, "It's the network piece—making sure that you know where people are and knowing the people in different agencies, and being able to call on them and say 'Hey, can you help me out? I've got some students….'" Another educator said that a co-worker

> pointed me in the right direction for establishing personal relationships with different key people within adult service organizations.… I promptly invited them to lunch and picked their brains. That's the biggest help for me: using the networking connections personally and establishing relationships with people so I can just pick up the phone and say, "Well, what about this?" and "What about that?"

When you value relationship building and collaboration, your attitude reflects this, and you begin to accommodate others more readily, learn their needs and limitations, and share resources. One special educator said that interagency collaboration "ultimately comes down to the personalities of the people involved and how well they're about to establish trustworthy relationships. When you have trusting relationships, then you're in business." An administrator summarized the benefits to strong relationships by saying:

> Once a community reaches that level [high collaboration], an outgrowth of that is you get to a culture of commitment and all of a sudden, agencies are making suggestions [to the school], employers are making suggestions, and it goes far beyond the scope of one individual. It almost feeds on itself.

In this chapter, you will see what it looks like when educators collaborate, both with other school staff and with outside entities (e.g., adult agency staff, employers, parents, community agencies, volunteers). You will learn strategies and see examples of how you can expand your ability to collaborate, many of which have been identified in research (Noonan, Morningstar, & Gaumer Erickson, 2008; Noonan & Morningstar, 2012). These strategies don't need to occur in order; you can do any of them at any time. They are designed so you can get started today.

Preparatory Activity: Reflect on Your Current Practices and Prioritize your Focus

Wondering where to start? Self-awareness is an important first step to increasing both intra-school and interagency collaboration. Intra-school collaboration refers to how well you work with other school professionals (e.g., school counselors, general educators, special educators, career-tech educators, administrators). Interagency collaboration refers to how well you systematically work with any and all of the relevant entities outside the school (e.g., vocational rehabilitation (VR), chamber of commerce, employers, parents, independent living centers). As an individual, it's important to consider your current practices and direct your efforts to address areas of need for your students and youth within your community.

Collaboration is more than a single act. It is not even just an ongoing process: it is a mindset. To become collaborative, you must first be willing to share your thoughts with others and listen to their ideas without judgment. The Transition Collaboration Strategies Survey (Figure 2.1; Noonan, Gaumer Erickson, & Morningstar, 2012; see Appendix, Tool #1) is designed to help you to assess your own collaborative skills. This chapter delves into each of the items on the survey, suggesting activities that you can do today and providing real-life examples of the strategies in action. After completing the survey, either read through all of the strategy descriptions and activities or jump to those that correspond with items you identify as high need.

mindset!

Figure 2.1
Transition Collaboration Strategies Survey

Tool #1: *Transition Collaboration Strategies Strengths and Weaknesses*

Purpose: This checklist allows transition professionals to quickly reflect on their strengths and areas of need as they work toward collaborating with their colleagues and other members of their community.

Instructions: Review each item, writing a plus sign by your areas of strength and a minus sign by areas of need. If numerous areas of need exist, it may be helpful to prioritize the needs.

+ OR -		TRANSITION COLLABORATION STRATEGIES
	1.	I have a clear understanding of how my co-workers' jobs are related to transition.
	2.	I have a clear understanding of a variety of adult agency services that young adults with disabilities may access.
+	3.	I feel that my boss supports transition education/services.
+	4.	I communicate information about transition to co-workers within my school/ organization.
	5.	I communicate information about transition to colleagues from outside my school/ organization.
	6.	I communicate frequently with families about transition planning and services.
	7.	On a regular basis, I coordinate transition services with co-workers in my school/ organization.
	8.	I regularly work with staff outside my school/organization to coordinate transition services.
+	9.	I participate in professional development related to transition.
+	10.	I participate in professional development outside my organization where I learn ways to improve transition practices.

Note. Adapted with permission from Transition Collaboration Survey, by P. Noonan, A. Gaumer Erickson, and M. Morningstar, 2012, Lawrence, KS: Center for Research on Learning, University of Kansas. Copyright 2012 by the Center for Research on Learning, University of Kansas.

Although it is beneficial to review all of the strategies in this chapter, it is most important for you to focus on those that directly correspond to your specific areas of need. Strategies in this chapter include:

- Strategy 1: Gain an Understanding of How Co-Workers' Jobs Are Related to Transition
- Strategy 2: Increase Awareness and Knowledge of Adult Agency Services
- Strategy 3: Gain Administrator Buy-In
- Strategy 4: Communicate Information About Transition to Co-Workers
- Strategy 5: Communicate Information About Transition to the Local Community
- Strategy 6: Communicate Information About Transition to Families
- Strategy 7: Coordinate With Co-Workers to Provide Transition Services
- Strategy 8: Coordinate With Agency Representatives to Provide Transition Services
- Strategy 9: Participate in Professional Development Related to Transition
- Strategy 10: Participate in Professional Development Sponsored by Community Agencies

Strategy 1: Gain an Understanding of How Co-Workers' Jobs Are Related to Transition

To effectively collaborate with other organizations, you must first understand the strengths and limitations of your own organization and begin developing a collaborative environment. Unfortunately, educators often feel isolated in their work, and experience little meaningful collaboration with their colleagues. Although the Individuals With Disabilities Education Act (IDEA, 2006) transition requirements typically become the responsibility of the transition services specialist or special education teacher, educators across all disciplines focus on ensuring that students leave high school ready for life (i.e., college, career, community living). Starting your collaboration efforts internally, within your school or organization, will support the development of a culture of collaboration and lessen the burden on you to lead all interagency collaboration efforts.

Activity 1.1: Interview School Personnel

In the general education and special education graduate-level courses that we teach, we always include an assignment requiring the practicing teachers to interview at least two school staff in roles different from their own. In other words, special education teachers cannot interview other special education teachers, but they can interview general education teachers, guidance counselors, career and technical education teachers, and so on. Having read the interview summaries and reflections of approximately 300 students, we are convinced that it is a powerful activity that builds a foundation for collaborative relationships. These teachers always report learning new information and understanding the perspectives of others more fully. In many cases, they identify methods to continue the discussion on an ongoing basis. They also often change their practices (e.g., communication strategies, instructional practices) and identify ways to support students in a more meaningful way through ongoing collaboration. This exercise is valuable for teachers at all experience levels. We invite you to connect with other school staff using the discussion prompts in the following paragraph to structure your conversation.

Discussion Topics: These topics are here to help guide your discussion. You can tailor the conversation to meet your unique situation. You can talk broadly about inclusion and serving students with disabilities in the general education classroom, or you can talk specifically about a student with whom you work.

- *Inclusion:* How to tell when students re successful in the general education environment, what to do if students are not successful, information provided in students' individualized education programs (IEPs) and how to translate that information into supports, strategies for working with students who exhibit inappropriate behavior.
- *Family involvement:* Typical means of communication with families of students with disabilities, strategies to improve or increase communication, strategies to increase family involvement.
- *Collaboration between general and special education:* Best ways to communicate regarding the progress of specific students, thoughts about co-teaching, supports that can be provided to assist with accommodations and modifications in the classroom, information that should be shared by general education teachers at IEP meetings, strategies for working with paraprofessionals.
- *Transition planning:* Ways to help prepare students for self-determination, independent living, employment, and postsecondary education (at the elementary level, this might be a discussion of teaching students social skills and decision-making strategies); how transition skills can be infused into the general education curriculum; assessments given in the classroom that support college and career awareness.

These topics are intended to help guide your discussion; you can tailor the conversation to your unique situation. You can talk broadly about inclusion and serving students with disabilities in the general education classroom, or you can talk specifically about a student with whom you work.

When you initiate these conversations, be sure to practice active listening. Active, effective listening means intentionally focusing on the person you are listening to, whether in a group or one on one, in order to understand what he or she is saying, and then checking for understanding (Landsberger, 2012, ¶1). "As the listener, you should repeat back in your own words what they have said to their satisfaction. This does not mean you agree with the person, but rather understand what they are saying"

(Landsberger, 2012, ¶1). Upon reflection after interviewing her general education colleague, one special education teacher wrote,

> We have so much in common. We both want to provide the best education to students and support students to reach their potential. I didn't realize that the general education teacher actually wanted more information about the students and wanted to provide ongoing progress updates. I thought I was doing my job by not asking the teacher to be involved at this level, but it turns out, not receiving or providing frequent feedback was making it more difficult for the teacher to meet the student's needs.

In another instance, the special education teacher learned that at every English department meeting, teachers described projects and lessons they had implemented, applying the content to college and career options. Although the special educator taught a modified language arts course, she had never collaborated with anyone on the content. They agreed that she would start attending the department meetings to learn about and share lesson ideas.

Strategy 2: Increase Awareness and Knowledge of Adult Agency Services

In order to collaborate across agencies, you must first identify the individuals or organizations that share a mission for improving the lives of youth with disabilities. You may already know a few of these individuals, but remember that individuals working with youth (e.g., teachers, community service agencies, family members) often do so in isolation. This means that there may be many individuals you have not yet met who could help you improve transition services. All of these people probably recognize that collaboration will support youth to transition from school to their desired postschool outcomes (i.e., college/continued education, employment, and community participation), but they may not recognize that it also can help decrease their individual workload in navigating the school to community transition.

Not all special educators feel comfortable interacting with adult service providers. In fact, many have reported that they have little understanding of or experience with agencies and adult services, and these teachers may not feel capable of supporting families through transition. However, research shows that effective transition activities are implemented by teachers who believe they are well prepared; developing a level of comfort with these services will help you feel empowered to provide improved transition services for your students (Benitez, Morningstar, & Frey, 2009).

Activity 2.1: Develop or Expand a List of Community Resources

To increase your knowledge of potential collaborative partners, we suggest utilizing or developing a condensed community resource map (see Chapter 3, Strategy 15), typically referred to as a resource guide. Resource guides simply list agencies in the community, the services that they provide, and their contact information. IDEA (2006) requires that, when appropriate, a representative of a participating agency should be invited to a student's IEP team meeting (34 C.F.R. § 300.32[b][3]). As a result, many school districts have already created such resource guides to help special education teachers and transition specialists identify appropriate agencies and adult service providers that can support students' postsecondary transition.

In Chapter 3, you'll learn about community resource mapping, but before the in-depth mapping strategy, it's helpful to simply list potential partners for collaboration. First, find out if a community resource guide already exists for your community. These are typically available in a local high school to support interagency collaboration during IEP meetings; if one exists, you will want to verify that the information is current. If a community resource guide does not yet exist, this book provides instructions on how to create one in Strategy 15. Use the guide as a basis for exploring community resources, but also seek out additional resources. You might even want to involve students in this activity through the steps provided below. While supporting your compilation of information on community agencies, they can work toward research and writing standards by formatting the information using correct spelling and grammar—and toward self-determination goals by identifying agencies that might be a resource for them.

If you need to create a resource guide, first make a list of all of the agencies you know that serve youth with disabilities in your community (e.g., VR services, centers for independent living, parent information and training centers, career centers, college disability support offices). Next, conduct a quick online search to identify other community service providers; you can search for statewide agencies or access the federal government's collection of resources at https://www.disability.gov/. Continue your list by adding additional agency names and web site URLs. Don't get caught up in this stage; a list of 10 agencies is fine at this point. Some agencies that are typically included on this list include:

- Vocational Rehabilitation Services
- Centers for Independent Living   VOA
- Parent Information and Training Centers
- Developmental Disability Organizations
- Career Centers
- College Disability Support Offices

Have other teachers give a list of community partners they interact with. This could be a foot-in-the-door for volunteer work. (community resource map)

A more comprehensive list of potential agencies is included in the community resource mapping strategy in Chapter 3.

Organize your list. We suggest simply organizing your list in alphabetical order in a format similar to the example below. Add additional information about the agency. For the resource guide to be useful, you will want to include contact information and a brief description of the agency's mission or services provided. Today, the majority of this information can be found online.

Share your resource guide with others and ask them to help you identify additional agencies. Consider professionals who may be willing to work with you to expand and share the resource guide. The first people you think of will often be from your own organization; expanding your collaboration skills with your peers is a great place to start. Starting and sharing an initial list is the beginning of a process to build and continually update a comprehensive guide for your own use and to assist others in your community.

Activity 2.2: Join Community Organizations and Committees

Like each community, local organizations (e.g., chambers of commerce, Rotary Clubs, Kiwanis and Lions Clubs, American Legion, developmental disabilities councils) are unique, but they typically have a common purpose of improving the lives of individuals in the community. Isn't that what you're doing in your profession as well? Becoming involved in these organizations not only fits your personal mission, but it also can lead to future collaborative efforts to support youth with disabilities. Some examples of local organizations include:

- Chamber of Commerce
- Rotary   *VOA*
- Kiwanis
- Lions
- American Legion
- Developmental Disabilities Council

As one educator who provides transition services explained, "We attend their meetings; we sit on some of the boards that they sit on…, we get to know them on a personal basis. I think that is probably the key." Once you have networked by joining these organizations, you will have a broader base of potential collaborators to draw from when expanding your efforts to improve transition.

Strategy 3: Gain Administrator Buy-In

Gaining the support of school leadership is key to expanding interagency collaboration. School administrators allocate administrative and staff time and resources to specific organizational goals. Common priorities for schools include increasing academic achievement, increasing graduation rates, decreasing dropout rates, improving community perceptions of the school, and improving students' postschool outcomes. When seeking support from school leadership, it's important to stress the ways that these specific priorities interact with interagency collaboration—especially collaboration focused around transition efforts. You also should keep leadership up to date when working on collaborative efforts.

Administrative support can include allowing flexible scheduling or compensating time and providing a stipend for summer training or substitutes when needed. As one educator who provides transition services noted, "When special education directors aren't involved, collaboration doesn't happen." Indeed, administrator support can be invaluable when trying to deal with the logistics of collaborative efforts. This support may result in the development of a memorandum of understanding, a formalized relationship between two agencies. For more information on Memorandums of Understanding, please consult (see Chapter 6, Strategy 26).

Activity 3.1: Present at a School Board Meeting

School administrators report to the local school board, and their budgets are often determined by board decisions. To engage leadership, it's important that those with decision-making authority understand the needs of youth with disabilities and are informed about strategies that simultaneously support the mission of the school and improve student outcomes. Presenting at a school board meeting is a great way to provide information about transition and promote your cause to your school district's leaders.

Figure 2.2 is a PowerPoint presentation delivered by a community transition team to their school board. The presentation outlines their objective, their partnerships, specific initiatives, and suggestions for how to continue improving the transition program. These types of information can be helpful to school boards. Be sure to celebrate your successes and underscore all the great work your team is doing, but leave the door open for continued improvement.

Roadblock Alert 1

As a member of a community organization, you want to be involved and form relationships, but don't feel that you have to say "yes" to every request for your time. Choose to be involved where you can best support your students and their future lives, and form meaningful relationships through depth (not breadth) of participation. In other words, don't spread yourself too thin.

ROADBLOCK ALERT!

Figure 2.2
Community Transition Team Presentation

Presentation to the Board
3/8/2012

Branson CTT
Tracy Hall Team Leader

The overall goal of the Transition Program is to help students develop the skills and knowledge to ensure a smooth transition through school and ensure positive postsecondary outcomes.

We make every effort to empower young people to transition from school to adult life as responsible contributing citizens by maximizing employment potential, independence, and integration into the community.

Figure 2.2
Community Transition Team Presentation *(cont'd)*

The BHS transition program provides assistance and opportunity for students to move successfully from high school to adult life.

A self-determination emphasis, with career-specific academics, and hands-on experiences are Transition Program essentials which contribute to postsecondary success!

Our current partners providing hands-on job experience on a weekly basis.

Loyd's Electric

Hilton Convention Center

Skaggs Hospital

L&J Plumbing

Harry Cooper Supply

Country Mart

Figure 2.2
Community Transition Team Presentation *(cont'd)*

Job shadowing experiences are designed so students play an active role in learning

Hilton Convention Center   Scaggs Hospital   L&J Plumbing

The Crow's Nest

- Students prepare and sell cappuccino, hot chocolate, and provide customer service.
- The Crow's Nest provides the opportunity for developing skills related to food service hygiene and safety, effective practices in money transactions, as well as, a setting for fostering strong skills in: work ethic; work quality; work rate; and communication and respect—skills valued by employers and transferable to all careers.

Figure 2.2
Community Transition Team Presentation *(cont'd)*

How to make the Transition Program more successful!

- Help students and their families think about postsecondary outcomes and identify desired outcomes.
- Design our school and community experiences to ensure that the students gain the skills and connections they need.
- Connect with more area businesses to provide a variety of hands-on job experience.

The Bottom Line

Too many students graduate to their living room couch, where their worlds become lonely and limited. Transition classes can help students find their way and be successful in life after high school!!!

Activity 3.2: Update Administration Regularly

We in special education often work behind the scenes to support students with disabilities Although this may work in some circumstances, it will not promote administrative support. Meet with your special education administrator or principal on a regular basis to pass on information about your progress in expanding collaborative relationships that support students' success after high school. In these meetings, learn about the pressures on the administrator and try to align your work with the administrator's needs. If increasing the high school graduation rate and decreasing the dropout rate are priorities, identify the potential benefits of intraschool and interagency collaboration to support this priority. For example, by developing linkages to community agencies, students will be more likely to receive supports that help them stay in school. A specific example of this could be creating work experience options with local employers to help youth see the relationship between school and their desired postschool outcomes.

By gaining administrative support and keeping your administrator apprised of your progress, you'll also develop an advocate who might assist you when you face barriers to collaboration. This is helpful both personally and professionally. On a personal level, you will have a contact who understands your challenges; on a professional level, you will have gained a powerful ally to help you organize and establish collaborative relationships.

Strategy 4: Communicate Information About Transition to Co-Workers

It's also important to distribute information throughout your school and district. As one teacher commented,

> We don't have the time as school teachers during the school day to get all the agency information out from inservices or conferences that we've attended. For us it's been important to make sure that we share and utilize each other's brains.

Although educators share a common vision of supporting students to become ready for life after high school, working in isolation hinders the transition process. No single person possesses all of the knowledge and skills necessary to ensure positive postschool outcomes.

Activity 4.1: Present to Co-Workers

One way to tackle this challenge is to follow the "train the trainer" model. After you or someone else from your school attends professional development training (e.g., regional or state conference, workshop provided by a community agency), share this newly acquired information with other staff in the district at an inservice training or departmental meeting. Discuss how the information influences your work and could influence the work of other educators.

For example, a teacher we know attended training on the topic of compliance in transition—namely, documentation of transition services on the IEP. She learned the information, but realized that many teachers at her school were not writing quality, measurable postschool goals. She asked the presenter for permission to use the PowerPoint and then asked her special education chair to present the information at the next staff meeting. Because she presented the information, her co-workers were better equipped to write measurable postschool goals for their students. Two co-workers even thanked her for bringing the information back to the team!

Activity 4.2: Provide Information in a Communal Space

Many schools have an intranet space where teachers can share resources. College and career readiness, a phrase that is frequently used in general education, could become a topical area for sharing transition information. As resources are developed, assessments are identified, and collaborative relationships are formed, this information could be disseminated schoolwide through internal sharing mechanisms.

For example, at a special education departmental meeting focused on transition compliance, the special educators all agreed that they needed to utilize a wider array of transition assessments to match the interests, preferences, and needs of individual students. They decided that for the next departmental meeting they would share transition assessments that they found to be beneficial. The guidance counselor also participated as a partner in transition planning, and shared a wealth of information and access to online assessments and college and career readiness tools (e.g., Missouri Connections, www.missouriconnections.org; My Next Move, http://www.mynextmove.org/; The College Board's Big Future, https://bigfuture.collegeboard.org/). Together, they created a large binder of assessments, organized by topic. They kept this binder in the teachers' lounge, which also happened to be the location of the copy machine, so that everyone could access the shared resource and easily make copies—distributing the information even more widely.

> ### Roadblock Alert 2
>
> If you are unable to gain administrative support, don't stop your collaboration efforts. Be sure to stay visible. It's tempting when you don't have administrative support to keep your head down and fly under the radar, but this isn't the best choice if you want to influence student outcomes. Instead, communicate your successes (even if for a few students), foundational knowledge supporting a program or initiative, and your vision for expanded services to administrators in your building, at the district level, and on your school board.
>
> ROADBLOCK ALERT!

Strategy 5: Communicate Information About Transition to the Local Community

Sharing information helps build a common vocabulary, provides an understanding of current practices, and gives individuals an opportunity to see the linkages between your work and theirs. However, sharing information only within your school will not be enough to substantially change the trajectory of youth with disabilities. As the saying goes, "it takes a village to raise a child"; you must communicate with this village to develop the collaborative relationships that will result in valued membership in society for youth as they exit school.

Activity 5.1: Develop an Elevator Talk

When meeting new contacts, it's important to be able to clearly and effectively explain the focus of your work—and being quick about it never hurts, either. This is why schools, organizations, and teams spend time developing their mission statement. Mission statements not only define the focus for the group, but also concisely explain the focus to others outside the group. So, if you were on an elevator, and someone asked you what you do, how would you describe your work? Keep in mind that you want to open the option for a future collaborative relationship. Here are two sample "elevator speeches." The first focuses on a single educator's mission, and the second provides information about a community transition team:

> Hi, I'm Sam, and I am an educator who provides transition services at XYZ High School. I help students with disabilities learn employment skills and find employment. In fact, I have had many employers tell me that the students that I have recommended to their businesses come into the job with better skills than most of the high school graduates that they hire. Here is my business card if you would like more information.
>
> ***
>
> I am a transition coordinator for students with disabilities in the XYZ Public school system. This past year, our school district recruited a dedicated group of parents, students, agency representatives, employers, chamber of commerce staff and other community stakeholders to create EMPOWER CTT. The vision for the group is empowerment for all students to achieve their personal goals and have success in high school and postsecondary education and employment, as well as being equipped with independent living skills. The ultimate outcome for our region is to create a diverse community that embraces the talents and abilities of individuals with disabilities, by helping them to be engaged within their community setting. Here is one of our flyers; it includes my e-mail address, if you would like more information.

Keep a speech like this prepared and ready to go in your mind so you can use it at every opportunity. Notice that both of these examples have common elements, which you should be sure to include as well: your job title or role, your place of employment, your individual or group mission, a major success that has resulted from your work, and your contact information.

Activity 5.2: Write an Article for the Local Newspaper

Your local newspaper (print or online, such as Patch newspapers) is a great resource for sharing information and requesting support. Newspapers are typically very interested in human interest stories of students or schools. The story could be a vignette describing one student's success, an overview of an internship or work-study experience that has been developed, or a call to employers for internship opportunities (see Figure 2.3). Personal stories about students' successes are great publicity for your team (provided you get the appropriate permission to publish them). The story outlines a students' own background, describes a program implemented by her community transition team, and explains how she has benefited from the transition team's efforts.

You might not always have access to personal success stories like this one. In this case, you may also choose to publish a more traditional news release covering one of your recent achievements.

Figure 2.3
Newspaper Success Stories

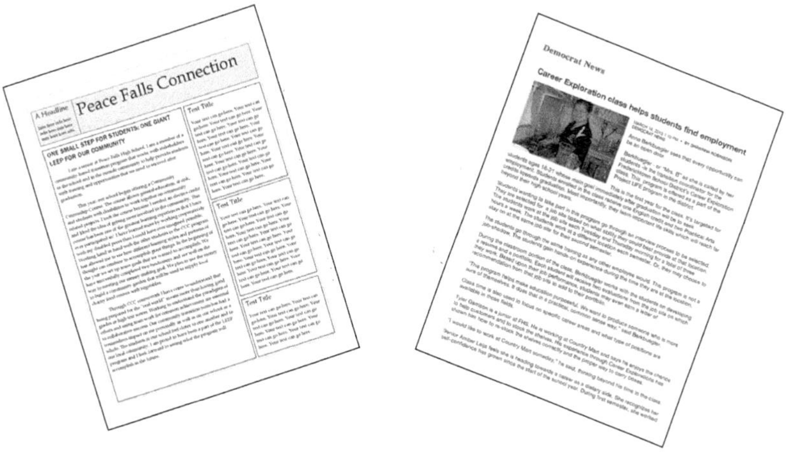

Note. Reprinted with permission from "Career Exploration Class Helps Students Find Employment," by S. Robinson. Copyright 2013 by the *Democrat News.*

Activity 5.3: Present to Community Organizations

Much like local newspapers, community organizations are often excited to hear presentations regarding the youth in their community, particularly if the students themselves present their experiences. This engages the members of the community organization—and it also can help students practice presentation skills. This communication often leads to further collaboration: After these other groups get to know you and to understand both your vision and your devotion to the successful transition of youth into the community, they are much more likely to respond positively to requests for support (e.g., presentation to a class, identification of work experience opportunities, booth at a transition fair).

Another option is to distribute materials asking for a community response. Figure 2.4 is part of a brochure created by a community transition team that wanted to increase employment opportunities for individuals with disabilities. The brochure lists benefits for the employers as well as a variety of ways they can get more involved. Interested parties check one or more ways they would like to participate, and return their responses to the team contact. While this example is from a community transition team, you could certainly create something similar to fit your specific needs. For resources that might aid you in developing information geared toward employers, visit the U.S. Small Business Administration (http://www.sba.gov/content/hiring-people-with-disabilities), the National Center on Workforce and Disability (http://www.onestops.info/article.php?article_id=55), or the U.S. Department of Labor (http://www.dol.gov/dol/topic/disability/hiring.htm).

Strategy 6: Communicate Information About Transition to Families

High-performing districts share the common characteristic of providing readily available information about adult agency contacts, types of available services, and strategies for securing, in formats that can be easily understood by both students and their families. IDEA requires that transition planning be part of the IEP process by the time a student turns 16 (or younger, if the team prefers; 34 C.F.R § 300.320[b] and [c]]). It is important that families begin thinking early on about possible adult outcomes and supports for their child; continuing the conversation throughout students' secondary years will help both families and students make a smooth transition. Simply providing a list of agencies to contact is insufficient, and does not facilitate the development of ongoing relationships between agency staff, students, and families.

There are many ways to provide information on adult agency services, employment, and postsecondary education to students and families. Consider incorporating information into students' classes, hosting agency presentations, and arranging experiences in the community. Over the years we have encountered several great examples of information dissemination: employer-provided biannual training sessions for students at a corporate

Figure 2.4
Community Response Form

EMPLOYER INCENTIVES

For Hiring Individuals With Disabilities:

- Tax Incentives
- High retention. Lowest attrition rate of any employee group in the country. (They complete their work and stay on the job longer).
- Increase pool of qualified applicants and productivity in all work groups because people with disabilities motivate other employees.
- Reduced cost for training, recruitment and turnover.
- Increase customer base and morale of all workers.
- Improve safety record; decrease accidents.
- A more diverse workforce appeals to a larger, more diverse customer base resulting in higher profits; 87% of the public prefer to give their business to companies that hire people with disabilities.
- High purchasing power of people with disabilities reduces number of families living in poverty and contributes to the local economy.

❏ Please contact me. I'd like to know more about the H.I.T. Team or how I can contribute.
❏ Count me on the H.I.T. Team! I want to contribute or participate.
❏ Be a mentor for a student exploring careers and employment.
❏ Host job shadowing at my place of business or agency/organization.
❏ Provide volunteer opportunities.
❏ Present work or life skills information to small groups of students.
❏ Consider hiring students with disabilities for part-time or post high school employment.
❏ Serve on an advisory committee: Promote the H.I.T. Team mission and how businesses and the community benefit from hiring individuals with disabilities and/or help create a program to make students aware of employment opportunities and skills needed to achieve successful, indpendent living.
❏ Attached is a note describing other ways I could contribute to the H.I.T. Team.

As a community leader your insight, influence, and involvement will crate a positive environment for all students to transition into being successful, independent adults. Your comments, questions, and ideas are always welcome!

THANK YOU for your time and interest in the H.I.T. Team!

---

site, mental health and independent living agency-provided life skills courses for students, and a university-sponsored 2-week summer camp for students with disabilities.

Just as there are different ways to educate students about community supports, there are many different ways to reach their families. Transition fairs, conferences, "field trips" to agencies, and agency-sponsored family trainings are all ways to disseminate information. School districts can set up evening workshops for families and agencies or host a monthly agency night. Offering child care for families during these types of events is a great way to promote attendance.

Activity 6.1: Disseminate Information to Families

Examples of informative materials developed specifically for students and families include: (a) agency resource guides, (b) manuals on navigating adult service systems, (c) checklists of potential agencies to contact, (d) a timeline of activities and linkages based on the student's age, and (e) lists of Internet resources for families. Information can be provided through interagency groups, local community centers, mailings, the school's web site, and presentations. For example, schools could send information on the transition process along with a mass mailing of report cards, or provide videotaped agency presentations that students and families could check out from a community room at the school or watch online.

Figure 2.5 shows part of a resource directory one transition team created for families. The directory includes information about transition, IDEA, assessment, IEP planning, self-determination, agency partnerships, and action steps for families. A directory of service agencies and a list of online resources are included as appendices.

A comprehensive resource directory like this one is just one way to get information to families. Another community transition team created colorful refrigerator magnets with information about some of their local adult service agencies (see Figure 2.6). The letter accompanying the magnet described the types of services provided by the different agencies.

(Letter Accompanying Magnet)

Dear Parent,

An open case with DMH/RO is the primary entry point for a student into adult services after graduation. Early enrollment helps to ensure that your student will have these services available after graduation and helps to build the bond between DMH/RO, your student and the family.

There are many services that DMH/RO can connect you with during the high school years:

- Respite
- Social skills training
- Summer camp
- Independent Living support
- Resource and referral
  - > Connect to services in the community
  - > Counseling, recreation, etc.
  - > Support with benefits (Medicaid, SSI, etc.)
  - > Coordination for PLB services

Figure 2.5
Sample Portions of Transition Resource Directory

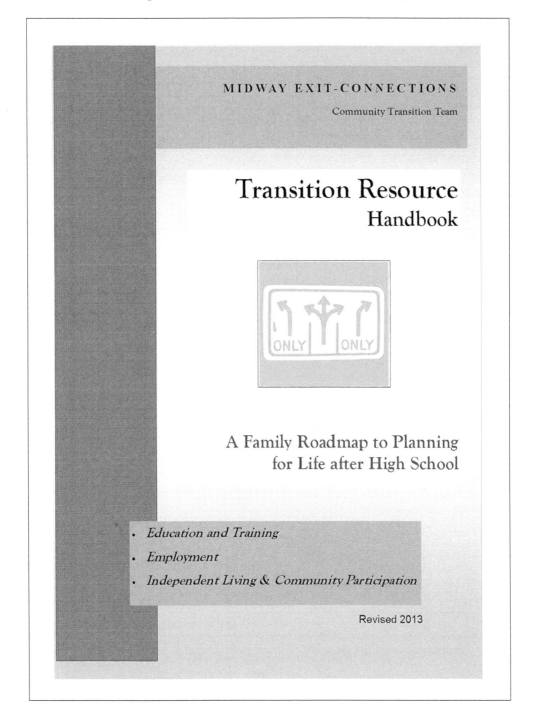

MIDWAY EXIT-CONNECTIONS

Community Transition Team

Transition Resource
Handbook

A Family Roadmap to Planning
for Life after High School

- *Education and Training*
- *Employment*
- *Independent Living & Community Participation*

Revised 2013

Figure 2.5
Sample Portions of Transition Resource Directory *(cont'd)*

Transition Resource
Guide

Table of Contents

What is Transition? 3
IDEA requirements overview 3
Assessment 4
Post-Secondary Goals in the IEP 4
    Education/Training 5
    Employment 5
    Independent Living and Community Participation 5
Self-Determination and Self-Advocacy 5
Agency Partnerships 6
What Can Families Do to Help? 6

Appendices

    A. Service Agencies 8
    B. Additional Online Resources 18

Figure 2.5
Sample Portions of Transition Resource Directory *(cont'd)*

Appendix A

Service Agencies

EMPLOYMENT & TRAINING

MISSOURI DIVISION OF VOCATIONAL REHABILITATION (often referred to as "VR")
http://www.dese.mo.gov/vr/transition.htm
Regional Office:
621 E. Highland, Ste 2
Nevada, MO 64772-3971
Phone: (417) 448-1332 Fax: (417) 448-1351   Toll free: (800) 598-3471
Tina Burns, Counselor
Raymond Drake, Supervisor
Vocational Rehabilitation (VR) and Special Education share responsibility in preparing youth
with disabilities for the transition from school to post-high school employment, education,
specialized training and independence. Depending upon eligibility, students may receive
vocational planning, career guidance and counseling, on-the-job training, tuition assistance,
assistance with finding a job, and independent living services at centers for independent living.

CASCO AREA WORKSHOP and Supported Employment Program (SEP)
1800 Vine
P.O. Box 506
Harrisonville, Missouri 64701
816-380-7350, Fax: 816-380-7363
Contact: Jennifer Palis: Jennifer@casco-aw.org

The Supported Employment Program seeks to develop and enhance the vocational skills and
talents of people with disabilities who choose to work in an integrated environment and to
increase their opportunity for meaningful life experience. The program works to assist clients
during each step of the employment process and to help them to be successful in a long term
vocational placement.

WEST CENTRAL MISSOURI COMMUNITY ACTION AGENCY (WCMCAA)
http:www.wcmcaa.org/index.php
302 Galaxie Box 9 109 Congress
Harrisonville, MO 64701   Belton, MO 64012
816-887-3850, Fax: 816-380-3043   816-318-3922, Fax: 816-316-3905

Youth and adult employment programs, as well as other support services for families in need.
Employment and training services include career planning, skill assessments, job search
assistance, internships and work experiences. Customers can receive scholarship and financial
assistance to attend certified vocational classes at local schools, community colleges or other
educational institutions in high demand, high wages occupations. Customers can gain skills
and experience through paid internships or short term on-the-job training. (There are WCMCAA
offices in many other regional Missouri counties. See web site for other locations.)

Figure 2.5
Sample Portions of Transition Resource Directory *(cont'd)*

THE WHOLE PERSON
http://www.thewholeperson.org/index.php
3420 Broadway, Suite 105
Kansas City, MO 64111
816-561-0304, fax 816-753-8163
toll free: 800-878-3037
Email: info@thewholeperson.org

The Whole Person is the Kansas City area Center for Independent Living founded in 1978. They are a private, nonresidential, nonprofit corporation providing a full range of community-based services for people with disabilities. The Whole Person assists people with disabilities to live independently and encourages change within the community to expand opportunities for independent living.

MENTAL HEALTH RESOURCES

PATHWAYS COMMUNITY BEHAVIORAL HEALTHCARE, INC.
http://www.pathwaysonline.org
300 Galaxie Avenue
Harrisonville, MO 64701
816-380-5167, Fax: 816-380-5841

24-HR Crisis Hotlines:

1-888-279-8188 in Johnson, Cass and Lafayette Counties
or
1-800-833-3915 in Bates, Benton, Camden, Cedar, Cole, Crawford, Dent, Gasconade, Henry, Hickory, Maries, Miller, LaClede, Osage, Pulaski, Phelps, St. Clair and Vernon Counties

Pathways Community Behavioral Healthcare, Inc. is a not-for-profit community mental health center providing a full continuum of mental health care and access to services in Missouri, including service coordination for clients who are developmentally disabled.

FINANCIAL & INSURANCE RESOURCES

SOCIAL SECURITY ADMINISTRATION-SUPPLEMENTAL SECURITY INCOME (SSI)
www.ssa.gov/disability
800-722-1213

SOCIAL SECURITY ADMINISTRATION DISABILITY STARTER KITS
http://www.ssa.gov/disability/disability_starter_kits.htm

SSA INFORMATION FOR INDIVIDUALS WHO WANT TO WORK
http://www.ssa.gov/work/receivingbenefits.html

Federal programs providing supplemental income, as well as work incentive programs, for eligible individuals with disabilities.

DMH/RO has but one responsibility with regard to employment of adults who qualify for their services, which is to provide retention services through job coaches after Vocational Rehabilitation (VR) has closed your student's case.

Here is a magnet with phone number you will need to reopen or open a case with DMH/RO. Please act now!

Figure 2.6
Sample Refrigerator Magnets

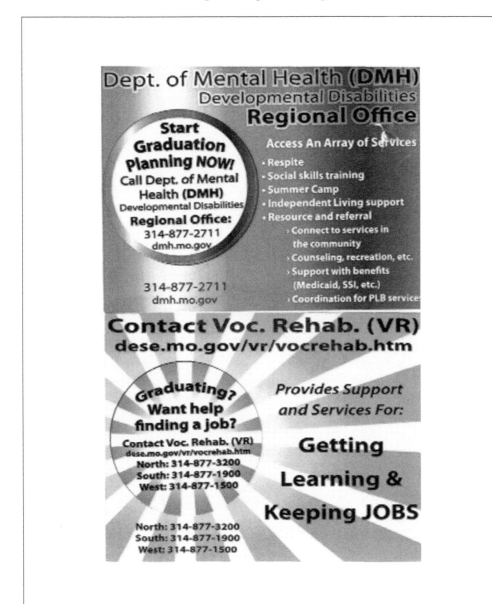

Activity 6.2: Facilitate Meetings Between Agencies and Students and Families

Effective transition planning requires establishing a close relationship between the adult agency and the student. As one educator who provides transition services stated, "We involve mental health…. When we're working out behavior plans, they're there. They now come to these meetings and want to come…. They are a part of it." When districts have deep, ongoing relationships with agencies, they have high levels of agency presence in schools, thereby encouraging student–agency relationships to develop. One educator who provides transition services noted that when adult agencies are in schools, "they know they're a part of what we're doing," especially as students move closer to transition and "the kids are getting ready to really be more independent."

Adult agencies need to meet with families as well as with students. Some educators who provide transition services help parents and students feel comfortable to ask questions by setting up meetings with adult agency staff in the family's home. In other communities, agency counselors spend one morning each month at the high school. This enables the special education teacher to schedule a counselor who can speak to classes, meet with groups of students, and meet individually with families and students regarding the services provided by the agency and how to coordinate transition services with the school. These meetings can be very beneficial for postschool outcomes; one educator who provides transition services emphasized that positive postschool outcomes are dependent upon "getting that relationship established before graduation."

Activity 6.3: Tour Local Agencies

Setting up appointments for groups of parents to tour adult agencies is also effective, especially in rural communities where individuals may have to travel distances to access services. One educator who provides transition services described her process of accompanying families to visit different agencies as an opportunity for parents to "start to educate themselves." Another noted: "It's pretty productive and parents are usually pretty anxious…. We block in some time for lunch and reflect on what we've seen." Touring local agencies helps parents to create linkages far more effectively than simply receiving a list of contacts. Once parents have seen how an agency works, they can understand its mission, envision how its services might benefit their child, and develop a rapport with staff that leads to a trusting relationship.

Strategy 7: Coordinate With Co-Workers to Provide Transition Services

The five stages of interagency collaboration are networking, cooperation, coordination, coalition, and collaboration (Frey et al., 2006). Up to this point, the strategies identified have primarily been at the networking level. When coordinating services, you're not just networking or sharing information: you're working together for a common cause. This common cause may not match up 100% with your personal mission. However, it's important that colleagues work together to advance their personal visions via a shared activity that they all agree is important.

We believe that data-based decision making is important to developing and sustaining collaboration and to obtaining the buy-in of multiple individuals. The first step in data-based decision making is to collect the data, and this is why this book includes a variety of tools and measures. The following activity will help you gather data about college and career readiness at your school, which will in turn give you a way to begin a conversation about collaboration with your co-workers. More information about data-based decision making is provided in Chapter 5.

Activity 7.1: Assess Your School's College and Career Readiness Practices

College and career readiness can be defined in a variety of ways. For our purposes, we define college readiness as the aptitudes, knowledge, and experiences that enable students to be successful in college or training programs. Career readiness comprises the aptitudes, knowledge, and experiences that enable students to be successful in entry-level employment that allows for advancement. The terms transition and college and career readiness are almost interchangeable; transition focuses on the movement from high school to life beyond, whether it is employment or postsecondary education.

The Indicators of College and Career Readiness Survey (Gaumer Erickson & Noonan, 2013; see Appendix, Tool #2 for a portion of the survey and www.researchcollaboration.org) provides a scale to focus high school staff efforts on curriculum, supports, and experiences that prepare students to reach their postsecondary goals. The survey has been reviewed and validated by three national experts in college and career readiness as well as numerous secondary general and special education teachers, educators who provide transition services, and administrators. Although the survey is designed for administration to all instructional staff in a school and then analyzed as a composite, individual teachers can complete the survey to focus their classroom efforts and identify areas of need that could be addressed through advocacy and in-school collaboration.

To demonstrate how this measure can be used, Figure 2.7 presents a section of the survey completed by one educator. (Data displays by domain area—not by measure item order—to facilitate easy interpretation.). Based on her results, this teacher has decided to attend a dropout prevention summit that focuses on student engagement strategies. She plans to share this information with other school staff and work to apply every lesson plan to a real-life scenario. Although she recognizes there are many areas for improvement, she has decided that she can implement this first step immediately and then identify additional actions she can take to improve her teaching practices and support her students to become college and career ready.

Figure 2.7
Sample Indicators of College Readiness

Indicator	Rating
14. I teach my students effective learning strategies that they can apply across content areas.	5 (4) 3 2 1
15. I teach my students time-management strategies and expect them to manage their time toward completion of multiday projects.	(5) 4 3 2 1
16. I teach and support students to utilize study & test-taking skills within my course(s).	5 (4) 3 2 1
17. I teach my students strategies for effective decision-making.	5 4 (3) 2 1
18. My instruction includes cooperative learning opportunities for students.	(5) 4 3 2 1
19. I relate my curriculum to our community (e.g., field trips, community-based experiences, guest speakers, discussion of community issues).	5 4 (3) 2 1
20. I adjust my curriculum and instruction around students' learning strengths and needs.	(5) 4 3 2 1
21. I support students to reflect on the quality of their work and ways in which they could improve.	(5) 4 3 2 1
22. Within my courses, students utilize current technology to complete assignments/projects.	5 4 (3) 2 1
23. Within my courses students identify real-life solutions to problems that have no one right/obvious answer.	5 4 3 (2) 1
24. Within my courses, students review and revise written assignments.	5 4 3 (2) 1
25. Within my courses, students apply their learning to their careers of interest.	5 4 3 (2) 1
26. I monitor the academic progress of my students through ongoing assessment.	(5) 4 3 2 1
27. I implement multiple types of assessments within my course(s) (e.g., performance-based assessment, short answer, essay, multiple choice).	(5) 4 3 2 1
28. My classroom assessments analyze students' higher order learning skills (e.g., analysis, evaluation).	5 (4) 3 2 1
29. I evaluate the effectiveness of my instruction based on assessment data.	(5) 4 3 2 1
30. I review data on students' knowledge and skills with other professionals in my school.	5 4 (3) 2 1
31. I review students' post-school outcome data to inform my instruction.	5 4 3 2 (1)
32. I collaborate with the school counselor(s) to support the college and career preparation of each of my students.	5 4 3 2 (1)
33. I collaborate with a transition specialist or special education teacher to support the college and career preparation of my students with disabilities.	5 4 3 (2) 1
34. I communicate with families on the academic progress of their student.	(5) 4 3 2 1
35. I receive coaching/mentoring to implement evidence-based instructional practices.	(5) 4 3 2 1
36. I participate in training to continuously build my skills in teaching my content area.	(5) 4 3 2 1
37. I participate in training to continuously build my skills in engaging all students.	(5) 4 3 2 1

Once a large group of teachers have taken the survey, their results can be combined and analyzed to get a complete picture of college and career readiness practices at their school. Figure 2.8 presents the aggregated results from 26 teachers from the same high school. Next are the results of the same survey section after it was administered to 26 instructional staff in one Southwestern high school.

Figure 2.8 shows a lot of data in a compact way. Each of the items on the survey is shown on the left side of each chart. The colored bars represent the percent of respondents answering with each of the various levels of agreement, which can be found in the legend at the top of the chart. The scale for the percent of respondents answering with each response option is at the bottom of the chart, while the scale for the overall average of responses is at the top. The labeled hourglass-shaped icons in each row show the overall average value of all responses for each item. This type of format can help you to quickly see trends in respondents' answers. For example, a quick glance shows that responses for the item, "Within my courses, students apply their learning to their careers of interest," are less positive than those for "Within my courses, students review and revise written assignments." Not only is the overall average lower for that item, but also there are far more "Occasionally" responses and far fewer "Regularly" responses.

These results reveal that the majority of the school's teachers are implementing many of the instructional practices that support college and career readiness. The school leadership team presented the results at a schoolwide inservice; all instructional staff agreed that they needed to focus on relating their curriculum to the community and collaborating with the school counselors and the transition services specialist to support students' college and career preparation. Each teacher agreed to identify a minimum of one lesson each quarter to relate directly to the community through a field trip, guest speaker, or community-based project. At the end of the first quarter, these lessons were to be compiled and discussed at another in-service training. The school counselors and the educator who provides transition services agreed to meet weekly during the first quarter to identify mechanisms to increase collaboration and information sharing. They developed a list of supports that they could provide within courses (e.g., presentations, assessment materials) and collected data on the college and career interests and skills of each student.

Activity 7.2: Identify School Assessment Practices That Support Transition

To supplement the results from the Indicators of College and Career Readiness Survey, schools should analyze their current college and career readiness assessment practices. In addition to mandated academic achievement assessments, school personnel need to assess students' occupational interests, aptitudes, values, and critical thinking skills to engage students in developing postsecondary goals and courses of study that enhance and customize their educational experiences.

In order to visualize your situation, use the assessment framework provided below. Here is one team's example: Through an interdepartmental team, one school in Arizona drafted their districtwide assessment framework to identify whether all students were completing transition assessments and were supported to analyze the results and make meaningful life decisions regarding their college and career choices. Below are the assessments that they identified.

High School Transition Assessment Framework. This framework is designed to support school teams in identifying schoolwide transition assessments: informal and formal measures that provide data related to postsecondary employment, education, and independent living. As with tiered instructional models, transition assessments should be considered part of the core curriculum for all students, with additional assessments provided for students with specific interests or needs. There are three levels of assessment:

- Core assessments administered to all students in a grade or core content course.
- Small group/elective assessments administered to students in an optional course or learning experience (e.g., career and technical education classes, internships, extracurricular, work studies/experiences).
- Individual assessments administered based on a student's stated/documented interests, preferences, strengths, or needs.

Figure 2.9 illustrates how one school compiled information on their districtwide transition assessments. Based on the draft assessment framework, the team realized that they needed to gather additional information from teachers regarding curriculum-based and performance-based assessments within their courses. They identified categories of students who were not being included in schoolwide transition assessments. For this school, these groups included students with moderate/significant cognitive disabilities and English language learners. They implemented a plan to simultaneously identify additional transition assessments being utilized by classroom teachers, determine the limitations of the core assessments for the identified student groups, and expand the framework to include additional assessments that could be implemented with individual students based on their interests and preferences.

Strategy 8: Coordinate With Agency Representatives to Provide Transition Services

In order to have successful interagency collaboration, you must work with adult service providers to build trusting relationships. To build these relationships, you must be sensitive to agencies' needs, limitations, and resources. Establishing these relationships has benefits for your school and your students. The most important factor in building relationships is maintaining a positive attitude toward collaboration. Adult agencies do not exist solely to serve your needs, just as you do not exist to serve theirs. Both parties must be aware of the other's priorities and needs.

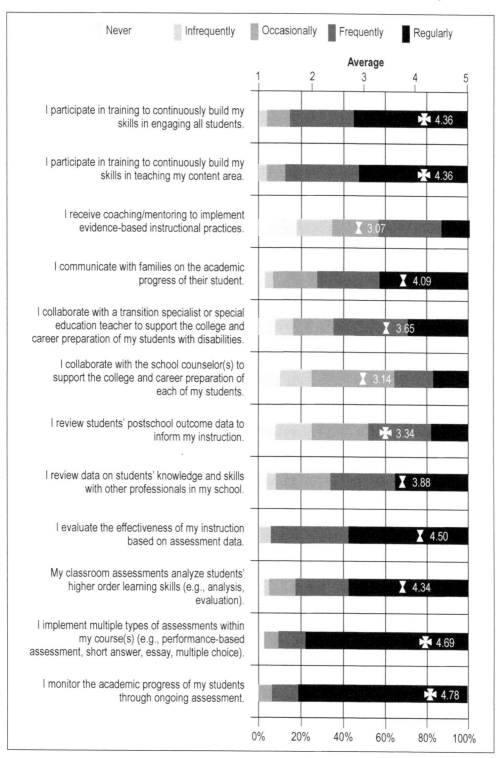

Figure 2.8
Sample Aggregated Results of College and Career Readiness Survey

Never Infrequently Occasionally Frequently Regularly

Average
1   2   3   4   5

I participate in training to continuously build my skills in engaging all students. — 4.36

I participate in training to continuously build my skills in teaching my content area. — 4.36

I receive coaching/mentoring to implement evidence-based instructional practices. — 3.07

I communicate with families on the academic progress of their student. — 4.09

I collaborate with a transition specialist or special education teacher to support the college and career preparation of my students with disabilities. — 3.65

I collaborate with the school counselor(s) to support the college and career preparation of each of my students. — 3.14

I review students' postschool outcome data to inform my instruction. — 3.34

I review data on students' knowledge and skills with other professionals in my school. — 3.88

I evaluate the effectiveness of my instruction based on assessment data. — 4.50

My classroom assessments analyze students' higher order learning skills (e.g., analysis, evaluation). — 4.34

I implement multiple types of assessments within my course(s) (e.g., performance-based assessment, short answer, essay, multiple choice). — 4.69

I monitor the academic progress of my students through ongoing assessment. — 4.78

0%   20%   40%   60%   80%   100%

Figure 2.9
Sample Completed Transition Assessment Framework

CORE ASSESSMENTS			
	Assessment title	**Information gained**	**When administered**
Employment	ASVAB	Aptitude and interests in military careers	Grade 10
	Arizona Career Information System	Work values	Grade 10
	Arizona Career Information System	Work aptitude	Grade 12
	Career Report and Presentation	Specific career knowledge and interest	Grades 9, 11 Language Arts
	Education and Career Action Plans	Postsecondary goals and courses of study	Grades 9–12; completed annually
Education/training	Preliminary SAT (PSAT)	Aptitude in reading, math problem solving, writing	Grade 10
	Arizona Instrument of Measure Standards (AIMS)	Aptitude in reading, writing, mathematics and science	Grades 10, 11
	Arizona Career Information System	College preferences based on interests	Grade 11
	C.I.T.E. Learning Styles Inventory	Preferred learning style	Grade 9 Language Arts
	ACT Compass	Aptitude in reading, writing, math	Grade 11
Independent living	Arizona Career Information System	Reality check of lifestyle preferences with desired occupation	Grade 11
	Fitness assessment	Physical health plan	Grade 9 Physical Education
	Human reproduction quiz	Knowledge of reproduction	Grade 10 Health
	Voting procedures assignment	Process for voting	Grade 11 Government
	Interest rate comparison assignment	Budgeting long-term purchases; comparing rates	Algebra I

Note. Adapted with permission from Transition Assessment Framework, by A. Gaumer Erickson, 2012. Copyright 2012 by the Center for Research on Learning, University of Kansas.

Activity 8.1: Connect Your Students to Community Agencies

If you're teaching students, you probably have already considered the benefits of asking community members to present to the class. Bringing in community service providers can educate students about the supports available within the community. To make sure the experience is beneficial, be sure that the purpose of the guest speaker is clear to both the speaker and the students, that students have been prepped for the guest speaker by learning some background information and developing a list of questions, and that there is follow-up with the guest speaker. This follow-up should include a thank you from the students and you. Guest speakers also help you, as the teacher, learn about the agency's services and develop an understanding of the agency. One teacher asked workforce center staff to present to a class on a quarterly basis. These presentations expanded into co-teaching a lesson each quarter on workplace skills. The students and teacher also learned about summer employment opportunities offered through the workforce center. Through this collaboration, more than half of the students applied and were accepted into the program.

Once students leave high school, they will need to access services when needed, but teachers tell us that students often do not know where to access services or what services they are eligible to receive. Giving a brochure or a summary of performance to a student or their family is typically not enough to create a lasting connection. Instead, to build a collaborative relationship, it's important for you as well as the student and family to interact with agency representatives, in person, preferably on their turf. Field trips will help you and your students learn about the agency and get comfortable within the agency's space. As with guest speakers, it's important to prepare both the students and the agency personnel. Students should research the agency in advance and develop a list of questions. Provide agency staff with a little background on the students so that they can tailor the field trip components to students' interests and needs.

> **Roadblock Alert 3**
>
> In rural settings, given the large distances between schools and providers, it can be difficult to connect students with community agency staff in a meaningful way. Consider technology (e.g., video conferencing via Skype) to facilitate virtual face-to-face interactions with adult agency staff, school personnel, students and families.
>
> ROADBLOCK ALERT!

Activity 8.2: Plan a Collaborative Project

Asking for help is an easy strategy to understand, but it can be much more difficult to implement. For so long, we have tried to meet all of the needs of our youth as individuals, whether as a teacher, parent, or service provider. To plan a collaborative project, you must be specific about the goal, set a specific outcome, and create a short-term partnership. A common collaborative project during the initial stages of relationship development with community agencies is a transition fair, where each agency sets up a resource table and is available to answer questions. Families and students browse through the fair, gathering information and asking questions pertaining to their specific needs.

One of the limitations of a transition fair is that it can be difficult to get families to attend. To increase attendance,

1. Provide child care. This could be done through family and consumer science classes as a volunteer opportunity for students.
2. Provide food. One community asked students to prepare and serve food. Because students were excited about the opportunity, families were more likely to attend.
3. Conduct the fair in conjunction with another event. For example, it could be held during parent–teacher conferences or alongside a college fair.
4. Consider the best time of day for potential attendees. Is it during the school day? After school? In the evening?
5. Provide transportation. Pick parents up at their homes, or transport a group of parents from one site to another.

Consider joint sponsorship of the transition fair, for example, the local center for independent living, developmental disability organization, and the school district may all decide to co-sponsor an annual transition fair. This approach not only lessens individual workload but also provides greater exposure for the fair.

Listening to the needs of families is also vital to your success. One teacher wondered why the attendance at the transition fair was so low. He asked a few parents of students with disabilities, and they explained that they weren't willing to share family circumstances and support needs in an auditorium with so many other families present. The next transition fair was modified to provide each agency a separate room with 10-minute meetings scheduled for families who wanted to learn more about the agency. Although this required more organization and advanced planning, families and agency personnel both reported that the conversations were more meaningful and led toward ongoing relationships.

Strategy 9: Participate in Professional Development Related to Transition

In addition to bringing other people on board through collaborative efforts to support students' postsecondary transition, it's helpful to continue to expand your own knowledge and explore practices that have been effective in other communities.

Activity 9.1: Attend Regional or State Transition Conferences

Most state departments of education offer regional or statewide trainings that focus on transition. Special education conferences, dropout prevention institutes, or leadership symposia also offer professional development opportunities. These are places where you will find like-minded individuals with similar roles as your own. The presentations will certainly prove to be informative, and many times it the informal interactions that have the largest impact on your local efforts.

Activity 9.2: Join National Organizations and Attend National Conferences

Staying current on evidence-based practices in transition is no easy feat. Joining national organizations such as the Council for Exceptional Children's Division on Career Development and Transition (DCDT) and attending national conferences can support your innovative thinking and provide the research base to justify your transition efforts. National centers such as the National Secondary Transition Technical Assistance Center (see http://www.nsttac.org/) or the National Dropout Prevention Center for Students with Disabilities (http://www.ndpc-sd.org/) also provide a wealth of resources and meta-analyses of recent research.

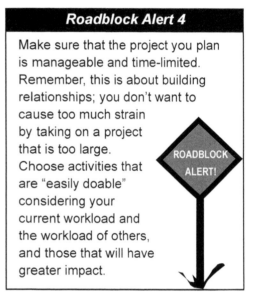

Roadblock Alert 4

Make sure that the project you plan is manageable and time-limited. Remember, this is about building relationships; you don't want to cause too much strain by taking on a project that is too large. Choose activities that are "easily doable" considering your current workload and the workload of others, and those that will have greater impact.

Strategy 10: Participate in Professional Development Sponsored by Community Agencies

Community service organizations often have their own conferences and professional organizations. Learning together with the local-level providers in these organizations can help you understand their systems, priorities, and vocabulary—which you can then use to improve your collaboration. Just like you, providers within community organizations typically need to obtain administrator buy-in for collaborative efforts. By learning more about their motivations, you can develop materials, presentations, or talking points that support advocacy for you and your community agency counterparts.

Activity 10.1: Attend Trainings Provided by Community Entities

So often, we don't consider the learning that is available outside our own area of expertise. However, for collaboration to exist, we must have an understanding of others' language, goals, and work. By attending trainings outside of education, you can learn innovative methods for supporting students to achieve their postschool goals. It also will help agency personnel to see how their work fits in with the work of other organizations. This common ground becomes the collaborative space for innovation and coordination of supports.

Consider this real-life scenario. A special education teacher we know attended a regional training for VR specialists. The training coordinator was surprised that she wanted to attend and mentioned that she might not get much out of the training. She explained that she wanted to learn more about their work and maybe get ideas for how she could work with students to prepare them for employment. At the training, she learned about a pilot project that was being implemented in another community: the VR counselor co-taught a junior/senior course on employment skills and obtaining employment with the special education teacher. At the training, the teacher also learned about areas of frustration for VR counselors:

> They want us to attend all of these IEP meetings, but we get no information about the student in advance, and many times when we show up, the parents and student aren't even there. It feels like they really just want us to sign the IEP stating that we attended.

After the training, the teacher met with a local VR counselor, described what she had learned at the training, and asked if the counselor would be willing to work with her. She proposed they begin by developing better ways for students and their families to connect with VR, and perhaps explore co-teaching a course through the pilot program in the future.

Although this teacher attended the training to expand her own knowledge, her attendance quickly led to collaborative efforts. The VR coordinator started coming for meetings at the school each month, which also helped develop relationships between the counselor and students and families. As the teacher related to us after several meetings, "Ongoing meetings have been extremely helpful to educate each other about what the expectations are in each of our systems. There was a lot of misinformation, and a lot of lack of information."

Conclusion

The strategies described in this chapter are designed to get you started on the path toward meaningful interagency collaboration. Although it is important to increase your own expertise and relationships, there are two important cautions:

1. You, as one person, can only do so much. To develop a smooth transition for all students to their desired postschool environments, others within the school will need to be well versed in available agency services, and everyone will need to understand the procedures for collaboration (i.e., when and how to communicate).
2. You alone do not make a sustainable system of support. Too often, when the collaboration leader retires, moves, or experiences a shift in priorities, previously developed collaborative efforts collapse. Sustainable collaboration requires a team of dedicated individuals so that other people with expertise can step into team leadership roles as needed.

To overcome these limitations, you can extend your collaborative efforts by developing a community transition team. The following chapters provide strategies for developing a community transition team, coordinating work within the team structure, and sustaining collaboration. With a collaborative mindset and willingness to try new strategies, long-lasting partnerships can be developed to enhance the postschool outcomes of youth with disabilities.

Chapter 3

Forming a Community Transition Team

With Jennifer Brussow

Chapter 2 described specific strategies for increasing intra- and interagency collaboration. However, individual efforts to increase collaboration are only the beginning. In fact, you will likely discover through relationship building that many agencies, employers, community organizations, and families share your vision for your students and would like to work together.

It can be difficult—and at times, impossible—for one or two educators to plan and deliver transition experiences for expanding groups of students. To solve this problem, many educators combine their efforts with others with similar visions to create a community transition team. A community transition team is one method to increase interagency collaboration.

To put it simply, a *community transition team* is a group of diverse individuals systematically working together to ensure that students with disabilities have opportunities to achieve their postschool goals. These teams are a mechanism for building relationships among students with disabilities, family members, educators, other school personnel, adult service agency personnel, employers, and community members. On community transition teams, people work together to develop a vision, common agreed-upon goals, and specific activities that improve transition opportunities for students. Although teams grow and change over time, they continue to promote structured collaboration between schools, families, adult agencies, and employers through purposeful, planned activities.

Community transition teams have been around for some time as a way to improve interagency collaboration. Their key function is to create linkages between educational and adult services organizations. The theory behind this model is that teams will be able to improve the capacity of schools and communities to deliver better services and help students secure resources to accomplish their transition plans (Benz, Johnson,

Mikkelsen, & Lindstrom, 1995; Blalock, 1996; Blalock & Benz, 1999). Because teams focus on services at the local level, they are better able to share resources and influence local policies and procedures (deFur, 1999). A community transition team supports the community's ability to help students transition by working to avoid service duplication and target emerging transition needs (Clark & McDonnell, 1994).

Although community transition teams look different from community to community, some common elements include:

- *Ongoing meetings*. Community transition teams meet according to a regular schedule, usually monthly, to develop ways to meet transition planning needs in their communities.
- *Established membership*. Members of the community transition team attend meetings regularly and represent the needs of the community.
- *Shared vision*. Teams establish a shared vision based on identified areas of transition need, and meeting activities relate to the vision.
- *Activity-oriented planning*. Community transition teams prioritize goals and carry out activities to support their shared vision for improved transition outcomes for young adults with disabilities.

Each community transition team has a unique set of members and a specific focus based on the community's areas of need, available services, and existing supports. Teams work on a variety of activities that share the end goal of improving adult outcomes.

When attempting to form a team, it's important to remember that collaboration is "a way of thinking and relating, a philosophy, a paradigm shift, an attitude change. It requires a set of behaviors, beliefs, attitudes, and values. The result is a sense of shared ownership, shared responsibility, and shared success" (Bishop et al.,1993, p. 11–12). To achieve this shared ownership, shared responsibility, and shared success, your team needs to create its own way of thinking and relating. Through your work with this team, you can create experiences for young adults with disabilities (e.g., employment experiences, college visits, transition fairs) to promote high-quality adult outcomes.

To assist you in developing a community transition team, this chapter presents six strategies:

- Strategy 11:   Develop a Community Transition Team
- Strategy 12:   Identify a Shared Vision
- Strategy 13:   Conduct Effective Community Transition Team Meetings
- Strategy 14:   Organize Your Community Transition Team
- Strategy 15:   Map Community Resources
- Strategy 16:   Enlist Community Members for Help

Strategy 11: Develop a Community Transition Team

In Chapter 2, you learned how to increase your awareness of potential partners and build relationships. After raising your awareness and initiating relationships with adult agency representatives, employers, parents, and community organizations, you are ready to take the next step—namely, creating a community transition team.

While developing a team may seem intimidating, take heart that many people share your vision and passion for promoting positive postschool outcomes for youth and would love to work as a team. Additionally, There are several tried-and-true methods that you can follow to gather the right people, establish a team, and begin carrying out activities to improve transition services. The first step is to identify like-minded professionals in your school or district who share your belief in the importance and need for interagency collaboration (e.g., transition services specialists, secondary special educators, administrators, career technical educators, general educators, guidance or counseling staff). After you have identified two or three school-based supporters, present the idea to an administrator, describing the benefits of the model (see Chapter 2, Strategy 3).

Next, meet as a school-based group to plan the formation of a community transition team. At this first meeting, your group should discuss community and student needs in more detail, identify potential people or agencies for the team, and plan the first community transition team meeting.

Activity 11.1: Determine Community Strengths and Needs

When school-based staff decide to form a community transition team, the first step is to consider the community's strengths and needs. *Community strengths* include things like established partnerships, involved employers, high levels of commitment from adult agency staff, community organizations, engaged parents, and strong teams. *Community needs* might include a high dropout rate, lack of employment for graduates, or high rates of school staff turnover. These strengths and needs are affected by a variety of factors, including your district's setting (i.e., rural, suburban, or urban), average student socioeconomic status, and history of past initiatives. In order to provide activities and events that will truly benefit your community, it is essential that your team understands, as a group, its strengths and needs. One way to determine community strengths and needs is to simply draw an image that represents your community—both strengths and needs—on a large piece of paper or a whiteboard (see Figure 3.1).

All communities have unique strengths and needs and can benefit from this activity. After discussing the community's strengths and needs in general, consider how these issues apply to young adults and adults with disabilities. For example, if the community lacks employment opportunities for youth, how does this relate to the need to teach

Figure 3.1
Sample Community Strengths and Needs Image

job skills and connect students with future employment opportunities? Continue this discussion for 20 to 30 minutes until all community strengths and needs are clearly identified and understood by the group. Table 3.1 provides examples of community needs and strengths from both an urban and a rural community.

Activity 11.2: Identify Potential Team Members

Although it may at first seem that there are limited potential partners, particularly in rural communities, teams across the country eventually have memberships ranging from eight to 10 people up to teams of almost 40. For the first meeting, it's important to limit the group to eight to 12 core people who have interests directly related to promoting positive postschool outcomes. Note that this does not exclude parents, employers, or community organizations; in fact, their voices and perspectives are critical. The general

Table 3.1
Sample Community Needs and Strengths From Two Communities

TYPE OF COMMUNUNITY	NEEDS	STRENGTHS
Urban	Diverse population (ethnic, international)	Vocational high school
	Large high school population	Small schools
	Varying socioeconomic status	Alternative programs
	14 feeder schools	District and school partnerships with colleges and community colleges, community organizations, city management
	Transient and homeless population	Team approach
	Emancipated minors	Job development and placement assistance
	Large undocumented population	Full-time release special ed facilitation
	Large geographical area (220 sq mi radius)	
Rural	Explosive growth	Commitment to cause
	Varying socioeconomic status	Growing communities
	Diverse population	Good relationship with postsecondary organizations
	High turnover at high school	Progressive
	Lack of infrastructure	Positive energy
	High freshman dropout rate	
	Poverty	
	Lack of family support	

rule is that an effective community transition team should include a wide range of professional representatives from community organizations as well as family members and students with disabilities. These diverse perspectives help to plan and accomplish activities with a strong impact. In your group of interested individuals, provide each person with a blank piece of paper and pen. Then, set a timer for 2 minutes. During this time, each person should list as many potential team members as possible (role and/ or person). See who can generate the most; then, combine all the lists for a discussion around the following questions: Who shares our vision and can help with the transition activities? Who do we need to recruit?

It's important to identify the agency or role for representation, but then you must also identify specific people (e.g., Bill Feehan at Walmart, John Green from the Chamber of Commerce). Consider your current relationships with people from these and other entities. Who do you already know who may want to be a member of a community transition team? When you are finished brainstorming, identify a small group of people to invite to an introductory meeting. Record the information from the group.

EXAMPLE

- Adults with disabilities
- Advocacy Organizations
- Behavioral Specialists
- Businesses
- Centers for Independent Living
- Chambers of Commerce
- Commissions on the Blind
- Community Colleges
- Community Center Boards
- Developmental Disability Advocacy Organizations
- Developmental Disabilities Organizations
- Departments of Health
- Employers
- Employment Contractors
- Family Preservation Agencies
- Family Members of Youth With Disabilities
- Foster Care Providers
- Housing and Urban Development Departments

- Juvenile Justice Advocacy Programs
- Job Corps
- Justice Departments
- Mental Health Organizations
- Native American Advocacy Programs
- Native American Colleges
- Optimist Clubs
- Parent Organizations
- Parks and Recreation Departments
- Probation Officers
- Rotary Clubs
- Social Services Leagues
- Social Security Administration
- SWAPs (School to Work Programs)
- The ARC
- Transportation Organizations
- TRIO Programs
- Universities
- Vo-Tech Schools
- Vocational Rehabilitation Services
- Young Adults With Disabilities

As you go about your day, be on the lookout for potential members, and have a short speech developed to recruit members. To work on developing your own elevator speech, look to Activity 5.1: Develop an Elevator Talk.

Activity 11.3: Invite Potential Team Members

In preparing for your first meeting, your school-based team may feel like it needs to have a clear purpose and vision already established—but this isn't the case. On the contrary, it's better to gather a group for the initial meeting and let the group determine if there is a shared vision and purpose to warrant the development of a community transition team. In other words, it's absolutely okay to not have it all figured out, and to let the group form naturally. This actually can build a more solid foundation for your community transition team.

For the first meeting, limit invitees to eight to 12 core people who have interests directly related to promoting positive postschool outcomes. Draft an e-mail explaining what a community transition team is and how your community, student, and agency population will benefit. Identify some issues or needs that your school-based group has observed (e.g., students aren't able to find jobs when they exit high school, young adults lack soft skills for employment, a large population of students with disabilities is dropping out of school). Then, extend an invitation to attend a meeting to discuss these and similar issues. You may want to develop a colorful flyer, and send it as an attachment to a very brief e-mail (see Figure 3.2). Because people may be hesitant to attend a meeting if they don't know the plan, it's a good idea to develop a brief agenda (see next activity) that identifies what will occur at the meeting, and include it with any invitation you send out.

Arrange to hold the meeting in a space where you can comfortably accommodate your guests, during a time that's convenient for outside entities. Pay attention to issues such as parking space and ease of access. Many teams hold initial meetings in neutral spaces that can be reserved for free, such as a library meeting room, basement of a chamber of commerce, hospital meeting room, or local restaurant; if you are considering sharing school-based resources with community representatives, you might want to hold the meeting at the school. If you plan to meet during regular business hours, schedule the meeting for no more than 2 hours.

Since people may be hesitant to attend a meeting if they don't know the plan, it's a good idea to develop a brief agenda that identifies what will occur at the meeting and include it with the invitation.

Activity 11.4: Develop an Agenda

Your agenda should include the start and stop times for your meeting as well as concrete timeframes for each individual component of the meeting (see Figure 3.3). The agenda should be drawn from the work you've already done to identify community needs and different organizations and individuals who might be stakeholders.

Roadblock Alert 1

Although it's tempting to involve a lot of people at this point, it's better to stay under 12 members for the first 4 months or so. This will allow the core stakeholders to build trust through jointly completing two to three activities. Once the core stakeholders have a clear vision for the group, integrating additional people will not complicate the team's development.

As you can see from the example agenda below, it's best to plan this agenda based on the strategies outlined in this book. The discussion of community strengths and needs relates to Activity 11.1, while the rest of the agenda is based on the activities identified in Strategy 12.

Figure 3.2
Sample Community Transition Team Information Meeting Flyer

**Community Transition Team:
Improving the Lives of Young Adults with Disabilities,
Enhancing Our Community**

Our mission is to provide collaboration, cooperation, and education for young people with disabilities, enabling them to successfully transition into adulthood.

Our goal is a smooth and effective transition for students, with outcomes that are positive and allow students to fulfill their life plans. It is important for students to be successful in life, believe in themselves, and be contributing members of the community.

Our model is a Community Transition Team, to improve community awareness and coordination and communication among service providers, employers, education concerns, and community agencies and organizations. This team will support students in envisioning their life after high school, and in understanding what they need to do to be successful as adults.

Our plan of action will be student and family driven, well developed, and goal oriented. To develop this plan, we need YOU — your insight, experience, and commitment to our community.

Please attend an informational meeting on **Friday, October 12, 6:00 pm, at the Community Center Meeting Room,** to learn more about community transition teams, and ways our community can help youth with disabilities reach their potential.

Please contact one of us if to RSVP or if you would like more information! We look forward to seeing you.

Denny Smith
Work Experience Coordinator
Rolling Hills High School
dennys@RHHS.bcps.edu

Claudia Hernandez
Senior Counselor
Rolling Hills High School
claudiah@RHHS.bcps.edu

John Cavanaugh
Vocational Rehabilitation
Belmont County
jcavanaugh@vr.belmontcounty.gov

Letitia Robinson
Employment & Transition Resource
Belmont County Public Schools
lrobinson@bcps.edu

Figure 3.3
Sample Informational Meeting Agenda

Community Transition Team
Informational Meeting
Thursday, March 7
11:00 am–1:00 pm
Greenbriar High School

11:00–11:15	Welcome and overview of community transition team model
11:15-11:25	Discussion of community strengths and needs
11:25-11:35	Personal and professional interest in transition
11:35-12:15	Debrief—Report Out
12:15-12:45	Establish shared vision
12:45-1:00	Discussion: next steps

Once you have created an agenda and distributed invitations, keep track of who responds that they are coming to the initial meeting. If people cannot come but are interested, save this information so you can keep them in mind for future meetings or team activities.

Activity 11.5: Hold Your First Meeting

At your first community transition team meeting, your main goal is to create a welcoming and collaborative environment in which people will feel comfortable sharing thoughts, ideas, and past experiences. As noted above, it is important to choose a neutral meeting space and provide attendees an agenda in advance.

From a school perspective, it is important not to overwhelm participants or send the message that the purpose of the team is to help the school. This is not the case; the intent of a community transition team is that all participants share a vision and care about the goals and activities. To this end, potential team members should feel valued and heard, especially at the first meeting. Some strategies to accomplish this are:

- *Limit the number of school personnel* who attend the first meeting to 30% or less of the whole group. For example, if 12 people are coming to the first meeting, then a maximum of four people can represent the school (e.g., school staff, administrators).

- *Facilitate the first meeting* to ensure that each participant speaks for a similar amount of time (not including the 15-minute introduction to the model). Ensure school staff members do not dominate the meeting.
- *Value the knowledge and contribution* of each attendee by listening closely and asking follow-up questions (e.g., how many young adults with disabilities are you serving now? What are your primary services?). Utilize the active listening strategies in Activity 12.1.
- *Adhere to the agenda*, especially start and stop times. To ensure that all members have a chance to speak, use a timer to keep the meeting on track. Projecting an online timer on a wall or screen is a discreet way to help people observe time limits.
- *Use process documents and activities* to accomplish your goals as a group (e.g., determining community strengths and needs; establishing a shared vision).

Remember the importance of involving parents in planning events and carrying out activities. Include parents as leaders on the community transition team, and listen carefully to their ideas and thoughts about increasing parent participation. It could be that changing the time, date, or location of an event could result in better attendance. Invite parents who are well connected to be members of your team, and utilize already developed mechanisms to reach more parents (e.g., phone tree, notes home with students, parent–teacher organizations).

Strategy 12: Identify a Shared Vision

Roadblock Alert 2

Never ask someone to join your community transition team prior to the informational meeting. It puts them in a difficult position to choose whether to join a group on the basis of limited information. Given our hectic lives, people need to see how their perspective is valuable, and how the group goals match their individual goals, before they commit their time and energy.

ROADBLOCK ALERT!

Strong, sustainable teams possess a shared vision and a common understanding of the purpose of the community transition team. Establishing a shared vision at the first meeting creates a feeling of connectedness and commitment to the team. It also enables team members to understand how small endeavors support a larger goal.

Bear in mind that school staff, adult agencies, local employers or businesses, parents, and other individuals joining the community transition team will enter the process with their own personal motivations and perspectives (*individual visions*). By exploring similarities and differences among individual visions, you should be able to identify a common thread. The following activity is intended to help you do this.

Activity 12.1: Identify Individual Visions

At the initial meeting, ask each attendee (including meeting hosts) to respond to the following questions. Each person should work individually to complete the following questions for 5 minutes. Then, each person reports his/her answers to the group. The group listens, and the activity continues until everyone has reported out (including meeting hosts). While people are talking, listen closely to identify differences and similarities (common threads). *Note:* All team members participate in this process when the team first meets. As new members join your team, have them complete the activity, too.

- What is your *professional history* related to secondary transition and interagency collaboration?
- What is your *personal history* related to secondary transition and interagency collaboration?
- What is your *vision* for youth and adults with disabilities in your community?

After everyone has reported their individual answers, discuss similarities and differences as a group.

Throughout this process, everyone at the meeting should employ *active listening* strategies; this helps people feel valued and comfortable expressing their positions, and also ensures that their point is understood. Active listening is an important part of effective community transition team meetings, and should be part of the way the team interacts at all times. However, active listening is especially important during times when personal information may be shared, such as relating a personal vision.

Active listening intentionally focuses on who you are listening to, whether in a group or one-on-one, in order to understand what he or she is saying. As the listener, you should then be able to repeat back in your own words what they have said to their satisfaction. This does not mean you agree with the person, but rather understand what they are saying. (Landsberger, 2012, ¶1)

> ### Roadblock Alert 3
>
> A lack of parent involvement presents a huge barrier to interagency collaboration. As educators, we depend upon families of youths with disabilities to help create linkages. One teacher surmised that parental involvement can be poor because "they're still grappling with the issue of disabilities and they just don't want to make the time" to meet with adult agencies.
>
> ROADBLOCK ALERT!

Strategies for active listening include:

- Before responding or questioning, express appreciation and interest in the topic.
- Briefly restate the key point to show you understand what the speaker intended.
- If you have a question, ask it in a positive, nonthreatening manner. If responding, state your idea, interpretation, or reflection, illustrating it with a fact or example. Invite a response.
- Maintain eye contact with the speaker.

To practice active listening in a large group:

- Follow and understand the speaker as if you were walking in their shoes.
- Listen with your ears but also with your eyes and other senses.
- Use your body position (e.g. lean forward) and attention to encourage the speaker and signal your interest.

This activity provides a way for team members to share their personal and professional histories as well as their unique visions for the community. The next step is to find the common threads among team members' viewpoints and establish a team vision. A team vision will not only guide the community transition team's main goals and activities, but also determine them. The vision will provide a direction for the group to ensure focus in the future. Community transition team visions should relate directly to the community's needs and strengths. A strong, concise vision statement will help outsiders understand the purpose of the community transition team.

Roadblock Alert 4

Don't be too narrow in your vision. A team needs a vision for the future that encompasses its goal and desired influence. Too often, teams try to scale back a vision; this can limit both creativity and effect. This is the time to shoot for the stars; do not limit future team activities to certain groups of students or activities.

ROADBLOCK ALERT!

When creating your team's shared vision, it is important to consider each team member's personal viewpoints. Activity 12.1 provides a way for team members to share their personal and professional histories as well as their unique visions for the community. Now, it's time to find the common threads among team members and establish a team vision.

Your community transition team is now aware of the team and the individual members' strengths and visions, but how will you get to a shared vision? Visualizing the goal through a group drawing is one way to help members arrive at consensus.

Activity 12.2: Create a Team Vision Image

When planning your agenda for your first meeting, allow at least 20 minutes for this activity; the goal is to create a collective vision for the potential effect of your joint efforts. The vision should reflect the common threads identified among individual visions as well as any additional ideas agreed upon as a group. Discuss the challenge first as a group to generate possible images and metaphors.

Figure 3.4 is an example of a community transition team vision image. The hand representing "school and support" is passing a diploma (representing an individual student) to another hand representing "choice and opportunity." The trampoline image (originally designed as a safety net) represents bouncing the individual back up into the process.

Activity 12.3: Translate the Vision Image Into a Vision Statement

After your team has developed an image of your vision, it's time to put the vision into words. Although this may sound simple, you should allow at least 20 minutes for

Figure 3.4
Sample Team Vision Image

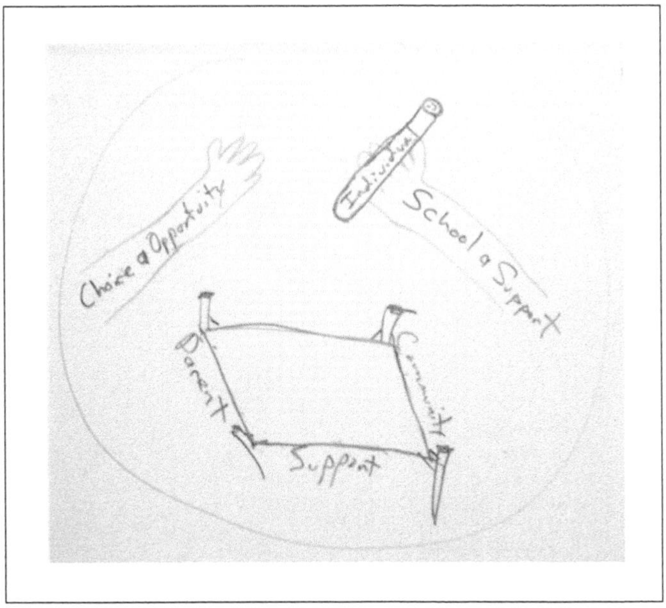

Note. Reprinted with permission from Missouri Interagency State Transition Team, 2010.

this activity as well. Here is a potential template for the vision statement: The vision statement should include the team's name, its purpose, its goal, the target population, and projected activities. Your discussion will be wide ranging, and should be centered on identifying strategies to improve postschool outcomes. This is the time to put those active listening skills to use.

Your team will use the vision statement in presentations and at your meetings, and it will appear on your agendas. It should focus your teamwork on your goals and activities while providing clarity, and also serves to validate and reinforce the team building that went into its creation. Figure 3.5 includes both vision images and their accompanying vision statements. See if you can identify the various ways the images and statements are related to each other.

A note about naming your community transition team: The name of your team should be specific enough to easily identify its members, yet broad enough to be inclusive of both current and potential membership. Because school staff often initiates development of a team, it seems reasonable to take on the name of the school or district. However, this may lead to other stakeholders perceiving the group as part of or belonging to the school or school district, rather than one that is representative of the broader community. The best option is to name your transition team based on geographic region,

Figure 3.5
Sample Vision Images and Statements

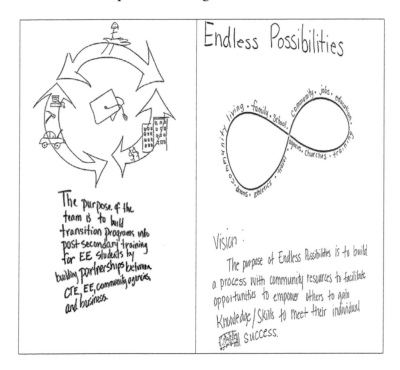

community, or purpose of the team, rather than after an entity or agency. This will contribute to the equality of team members and promote a spirit of inclusiveness.

Strategy 13: Conducting Effective Community Transition Team Meetings

13

To facilitate well-organized meetings, it's important to have structures in place about who will do what and how meetings will be run.

Activity 13.1: Assign Rotating Roles

To facilitate a well-organized meeting, it's important to have some structure in place about who will do what and how meetings will be run. Many teams assign specific roles for meeting participants to ensure that meetings are well organized and productive (e.g., facilitator, note taker, time keeper). These roles aren't set in stone; they can change meeting to meeting. Here are some suggested roles that can be filled by anyone at a meeting:

- Facilitator, whose responsibility is to adhere to the agenda topics, promote active listening, assess consensus, and ensure meeting is productive and on track.
- Note-taker, whose responsibility is to take and keep accurate notes of meetings.
- Time-keeper, whose responsibility is to hold the team to its agenda schedule and make sure meetings start and end on time. It can often be helpful to select people to fill these roles who are not the leaders of the community transition team, and rotate responsibilities to promote shared leadership and joint participation.

Activity 13.2: Establish Meeting Norms

It is important to establish meeting norms and guidelines at the first team meeting in order to ensure that all members are aware of the norms and to build consistency between meetings. When setting norms, use consensus-building activities to give members practice working as a team and help members feel that they are included and valued and include all members' perspectives. Consensus-building exercises give members practice working as a team and help members feel that they are included and valued. The following activity is one way to ensure all members' voices are heard while establishing a representative meeting norm.

Distribute an equal number of identical sticky notes to each member (ensuring the sticky notes are identical encourages anonymity). Ask members to reflect on the past three meetings (not necessarily community transition team meetings, but any meeting) they have attended and list their annoyances from those meetings. Each member should provide between one and five problems they have experienced in past meetings (e.g., leadership arriving late to meetings, meetings frequently being canceled or rescheduled, off-topic conversations that derail meetings).

Have members gather around a conference table and stick their sticky notes randomly around its surface (again, this promotes anonymity). As a group, organize the sticky notes by topic (e.g., attendance, start and stop times, meeting focus). Then, work as a group to write guidelines based on these categories. Make sure to phrase guidelines positively; instead of "No one comes late," use "All members arrive on time." Some examples of guidelines are:

- Sidebar conversations last less than 5 minutes.
- Each member attends at least 80% of meetings.
- Leadership arrives 5 minutes early.
- All members arrive within 5 minutes of the designated start time.
- All members stay until the end and use active listening.
- Note takers keep group notes in a team binder.
- All members are respectful of other people's points of view.

Roadblock Alert 5

It's normal to occasionally experience frustrations with lack of attendance, people arriving late, and lack of adherence to task lists, but it's never too late to establish norms. Your team can repeat this activity as often as necessary to promote healthy meetings with satisfied team members.

ROADBLOCK ALERT!

Your team should aim for approximately eight guidelines. Once these norms are established, they should be posted at every meeting. Some teams bring a poster-sized list of their guidelines to each meeting, whereas others list the guidelines on the reverse side of each member's name tent.

For norms to be successful, they must be accompanied by accountability measures. For example, if a member arrives more than 5 minutes late, he or she must bring treats to the next meeting; if a sidebar conversation has continued for more than 5 minutes, members may toss a communal stuffed animal to alert the speaker; instead of canceling a meeting, members will work together to reschedule at an alternate time. Norms must be followed consistently and enforced fairly. Correct use of meeting norms will leave all members feeling empowered and more satisfied with the way meetings are conducted.

Activity 13.3: Use Agendas and Minutes

Although agendas and minutes may seem overly formal and at times unnecessary, they are a valuable strategy for increased collaboration. We have all had the experience where we get busy in our work and forget activities and tasks we've agreed to address, especially if it's over and above our main workload. Agendas and minutes are essential to making sure the work gets done as intended.

A few things to note about agendas (see Appendix, Tool #4 for template):

- Agendas should be developed and e-mailed or mailed to all team members prior to the meeting. People are more likely to attend a meeting if they know what will be discussed.
- Agendas should include start and stop times, location of meeting, and topics to be addressed.
- Agendas should include a specific time for discussion, as team members will want to voice thoughts and contribute to work.
- Include the team vision statement, as well as important upcoming dates (meeting times for the year).

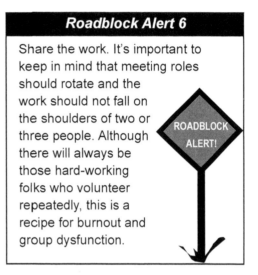

Roadblock Alert 6

Share the work. It's important to keep in mind that meeting roles should rotate and the work should not fall on the shoulders of two or three people. Although there will always be those hard-working folks who volunteer repeatedly, this is a recipe for burnout and group dysfunction.

ROADBLOCK ALERT!

Meeting minutes are also very important to the structure and function of a community transition team. Many teams use the meeting agenda to develop minutes, and they type notes throughout the meeting into this document. When taking notes during a meeting, it's important to record enough information that anyone who reads the minutes, even members who did not attend, will understand what was discussed and agreed upon. Summarize the main points of conversations, even if members disagree. Record the agreement. At the bottom of the minutes, include a to-do list that includes the task, the person responsible, and the target date. After the note taker completes the notes, send them out electronically as soon as possible to all members. Minutes keep members that could not attend informed and somewhat involved, and remind those who did attend of what was discussed and any tasks and deadlines they might have.

Strategy 14: Organize Your Community Transition Team

14

Activity 14.1: Assign Permanent Roles to Participants

When assigning permanent roles, remember that effective transition teams must have established leadership to ensure the overall functioning and existence of the team. One role you must assign is a leader, in the form of a chair or two co-chairs; this "permanent" role should rotate annually or biannually. Although it's tempting to have a school representative as the chairperson, it is recommended that at least two people share a leadership role on a community transition team, and it's best if one of the leaders comes from outside the school setting.

Team leaders have responsibility for ensuring the team functions, but they do not necessarily have to be the ones scheduling the meetings, developing agendas, taking and distributing minutes, or facilitating team meetings; these tasks rotate among team members. The role of the team leader is to oversee the teaming process to be sure that critical steps are accomplished—thus, the need for a chairperson. Chairpersons should change periodically to prevent burnout and overtasking one or two individuals.

Your team also will need to assign members to committees and subcommittees. Committees and subcommittees exist to work on specific tasks your organization wants to pursue, and name chairs for these committees. There are two types of committees: standing committees and working committees.

Standing committees exist to address long-term projects or concerns. For example, if you will be hosting an annual transition fair, then the transition fair committee would be a standing committee. Just because a committee exists indefinitely, however, doesn't mean its members are locked in for life. Committee members should rotate through standing committees so that no one becomes bored or burned out. Rotating half of the members out of the committee each year is a good idea and ensures that the committee includes both experienced veterans who can offer guidance based on the previous year, but you also get members with new ideas and perspectives.

Working committees are short-term structures formed to address time-limited issues. For example, if you are planning a one-time activity, such as community resource mapping (see Chapter 4), you would form a temporary team to complete that project. The committee meets regularly while the project is underway, but disbands after the project is completed.

Within all team structures, remember the importance of distributing the workload between team members. Unevenly divided work may cause certain members to feel overworked, and other members may feel unhelpful. Adopting *shared leadership* practices can ensure sustainability and encourage a collaborative climate. Although it is possible for a project to thrive under the guidance of a single exceptional leader, this approach makes improvements less sustainable. If the leader leaves, the resulting turnover can easily derail the project (Lambert, 2002; Timperley, 2005). If other team members have never had leadership responsibilities, they may be unable to fill the leader's shoes, and progress will stop or even reverse. In addition, top-down leadership fails to tap into team members' unique talents. Each member of your community transition team has strengths or useful skills to contribute. By distributing leadership responsibilities among members, your team can assign duties to ensure maximum efficacy and an efficient use of your human resources.

Adopting shared leadership practices doesn't mean your team can no longer have a leader or committee chairs. Shared leadership requires a different view of leadership, wherein leadership responsibilities are emergent rather than fixed (Gronn, 2000). In other words, when a specific task requiring leadership functions arises, the person who is best suited to that leadership role should take over the leadership practices for that task. As your team develops shared leadership practices, it may be helpful to consider the five domains of shared leadership set forth by Poff & Parks (2010, p. 32): collaboration, common focus, shared responsibility, supportive culture, and widespread communication.

In order to achieve shared leadership, your team must work toward achieving the goals within these domains. Although some of these domains can be accomplished in team meetings (e.g., common focus, shared responsibility, and widespread communication), other elements rely on individual and team values (e.g., Collaboration and Supportive Culture). These cultural values require a new view of leadership: rather than the traditional model of one leader possessing authority over the group, leadership should be a shared process of learning together and constructing knowledge collaboratively (Harris, 2003).

When implementing shared leadership, it's important to consider the differences and similarities of formal and informal leadership. Every group needs formal leaders such as chairs and committee heads to deal with big-picture responsibilities and make sure the group stays on track to its overarching mission. However, many people fail to consider the role of informal leaders when thinking about leadership functions. Any member can act as an informal leader, regardless of formal title (or lack thereof). Informal leadership occurs whenever a team member deals with day-to-day functions such as planning, communicating goals, regulating activities, creating a pleasant environment, and motivating team members. Though formal leaders also can take on informal leadership responsibilities, informal leadership may not be officially recognized. In fact, Spillane and Healey (2010) found that the majority of people with informal leadership responsibilities were not identified as formal leaders. Informal leadership functions are essential to efficient group functioning, so don't neglect them in your transition team.

> ### Roadblock Alert 7
>
> Shared leadership requires formal leaders to relinquish some of their power to informal leaders. Though some formal leaders will be happy to share work, others may feel they are being forced to "give up" power. Formal leaders may also worry about the ability of other team members to accomplish the leadership tasks that have been delegated to them.
>
> **ROADBLOCK ALERT!**

To encourage formal leaders to share power, work on cultivating an atmosphere of group trust. Formal leaders who know and accept team members' strengths and skills should feel comfortable delegating tasks. Shared leadership also reduces formal leaders' workload by more evenly distributing responsibilities among group members. If informal leaders can assume some of the day-to-day responsibilities, formal leaders can focus their attention on big-picture issues. Though resistance from formal leaders can be difficult to overcome, most will recognize the benefits of delegating informal leadership functions to specially qualified team members.

By assigning leadership functions through a collaborative process, members will be aware and informed of their specific responsibilities. This process also allows for the most efficient use of human resources.

Shared leadership has the potential to improve your team's collaboration, increase sustainability, and boost efficiency. However, it is important to implement the process carefully and deliberately in order to avoid misalignment of goals and values within your group. By distributing responsibilities, your transition team can improve its outcomes and overcome the negative impact of administrative turnover. (Chapter 4 will provide some guidelines on assessing the shared leadership of your group.)

Strategy 15: Map Community Resources

Another strategy for helping your community transition team function effectively is community resource mapping (Crane & Mooney, 2005; Ferber, Pittman, & Marshall, 2002). When determining how to best meet the transition needs of youths with disabilities in your community, it is important to have a strong grasp of the assets and resources available as well as what gaps exist. *Community resource mapping* is a process in which team members systematically gather information on community agencies and services in order to construct an image of the community's situation. This process can be adapted to focus on different areas, and it may need to be conducted multiple times during your transition team's lifetime. The steps listed below should be carried out each time the team decides to map community resources.

Community resource mapping provides a means to gain in-depth information about services, identify opportunities and challenges for your team's mission, and provide opportunities for policy recommendations and interagency collaboration. It can also help you:

- Identify new resources to develop, enhance, and sustain goals.
- Determine whether existing resources are being used effectively to achieve expected outcomes.
- Improve alignment and coordination of resources.
- Enhance coordination and collaboration among stakeholders with relevant resources.
- Develop new policies and legislation to better meet goals and objectives (Crane & Mooney, 2005).

Activity 15.1: Create a Community Resource Map

The first step in community resource mapping is to identify the specific area of need to research. Although "postsecondary transition" may seem to be a specific need, your team should work to target its search even more precisely. Examples of appropriately narrow areas of need include employment services for young adults, services that provide employment experience, and services that provide vocational training.

As a group, brainstorm a list of known services that relate to the identified area of need. Be sure to consider local, regional, and state agencies as well as services offered in the school system. Assign each team member to investigate one or more agencies. This work should be distributed as evenly as possible, and should capitalize on members' existing relationships. You will need to collect information on each agency's policies, procedures, funding, collaborative practices, services which relate to your identified area of need, and possibilities for interagency collaboration. Your team can decide whether members should collect additional information.

Once all information is collected, work as a group to combine your results. You might create a large table with the results of all agencies, develop a list of all services provided, or create a grid of available services to visualize agency overlap. From the combined results, identify any gaps in services. For example, you may have investigated employment services for young adults and discovered that dropouts are underserved by existing resources. Though some students drop out of school with the intention of finding work, there may not be services targeted towards helping 15- and 16-year-olds find work, thus leading to a large number of unoccupied dropouts.

After identifying gaps, your team should discuss how to best fill those gaps. Is there a way to expand existing services to fill those needs? Which agency or agencies would be best

Roadblock Alert 8

You may also encounter challenges surrounding compensation—or more specifically, lack of compensation for an increased workload. Without compensation or overt recognition, it may be difficult to motivate members to accept leadership responsibilities. To this end, your team should consider how to recognize both formal and informal leaders. This recognition can be as simple as a quick shout-out to leaders at the beginning or end of meetings or as elaborate as an official recognition ceremony. Be sure that all leadership responsibilities are acknowledged in some way. Consider incorporating this into your team's by-laws and meeting norms.

suited to providing these new services? How can your team work with these agencies to accomplish this goal? If there is no way to expand existing services, should a new agency be created? How could the transition team go about creating this agency or assisting with its creation?

As the result of an activity just like this, the Special School District of St. Louis County, Missouri (2012), developed a comprehensive resource guide for students with disabilities and their families (see Figure 3.6 for sample page). In addition to names and contact information, the resource guide includes a brief description of over 100 agencies and supplemental tools for students and families to support their use of the guide. The guide is organized into the domains of support services and advocacy, financial concerns, employment/training, day activities or volunteer programs, postsecondary education, living arrangements, social leisure/recreation, transportation, and additional resources.

The resource mapping process can be used for many purposes; your team may decide to widen or refine the scope of its goal, the level of investigation (e.g., local, regional, state, national), or the types of information to be collected. Resource mapping may also be used within schools to identify academic opportunities for targeted groups of students. In any situation, resource mapping is a valuable tool to identify, link, and align existing services while identifying gaps and planning improvements.

Strategy 16: Enlist Community Members for Help

One way to enlist community members to help with your activities is to host a purposeful gathering of community members. When your team is feeling overwhelmed or in need of new members or increased support, one strategy is to host a community conversation. *Community conversations* (Carter et al., 2009) are exactly that: planned events where many different types of people from a community gather to discuss a question or topic. These events attract diverse expertise and opinions and allow others to express their ideas and thoughts. It is not surprising that when people gather, express feelings, and feel heard, they are more willing to continue problem solving and could join the team or at least volunteer on occasion. This can be a great way to rejuvenate a team or increase enthusiasm.

Activity 16.1: Host a Community Conversation

To host a community conversation, first develop an invitation. The invitation should feature the discussion topic(s); plan for a 1- to 2-hour conversation in a neutral place (just as with the transition team informational meeting, someplace other than the school). Spread the word widely, using e-mail, phone trees, student notes, newspaper announcements, signs in public places, and word of mouth. Ask people to RSVP; when they respond, ask them to invite two or three additional people. Your goal is over 15 but under 100 participants; these events can occur with any number of participants.

Figure 3.6
Sample Resource Guide Page

ADAPT of Missouri, Inc.
www.adaptusa.com
2301 Hampton
Sf. Louis, MO 63139
1-888-657-3201

Provides supported living and psychosocial rehabilitation services to adults with serious and persistent mental illnesses.

ADAPT St. Louis
www.adapt.org

ADAPT St. Louis is an arm of national ADAPT, a grassroots, nonprofit disability rights organization advocating for equal rights and equal access for all people with disabilities.

Adapt-Ability Incorporated
9355 Oielman Industrial Drive
Olivette, MO 63132
314-432-1101
www.adapt-ability.org

Provides home, job, and equipment modifications. Also assists in finding funding for equipment and design fabrication of custom equipment, assistive communication training and computer assistance.

ADDAM
(Attention Deficit Disorders Association of Missouri)
St Louis Bread Co.
10741 Sunset Hills Plaza
Kirkwood, MO 63127
314-963-4655

Support group for adults, their families, and friends. Meets the second Thursday of the month from 7:30 to 9:30 p.m., October through May.

Advocates for Family Health
4232 Forest Park Ave.

St. Louis, MO 63108
314-534-1263
1-800-444-0514, ext.1251
Hotline: 314-534-1263
www.lsem.org

Advocates for Family Health provide assistance to children, families, and pregnant women who are eligible for Missouri's Medicaid program, which is now called Mo HealthNet. The project also assists people with a range of Medicaid eligibility matters, such as denials of application for benefits, wrongful termination of benefits and problems with payment of premiums.

Albert Pujols Wellness Center for Adults with Down Syndrome
St. Luke's Hospital
Mr. & Mrs. Theodore P. Deslodge. Jr
Outpatient Center
121 St Luke's Center Dr .• Suite 500

Chesterfield, MO 63017
314-576-2300
ADS. WellnessCenter@stlukes.stl.com

Patients 17 years of age or older will access the Center by making an initial appointment. After a physical, patients will be referred to various services focused on nutrition, exercise, safety and social/emotional well-being, specifically designed for adult Down syndrome patients.

When considering people to invite, think outside the box! Depending on the topic, you may want to invite:

- 4-H, Girl and Boy Scouts, and other youth organizations
- Boys and Girls Club staff
- Business and civic volunteer groups
- Chamber of commerce
- Citizen advocacy groups
- Mayor and city council (or county officials)
- College or university faculty and staff
- College students
- Community arts center staff
- Community gardens staff
- Employers
- Local cooperatives
- Local and state policy makers
- Media (radio, TV, newspaper)
- Public library staff

The meeting room should be welcoming; set up multiple round tables that seat about eight people each, to encourage conversation; put a notepad of paper on each table for people to use, and a table tent or handouts that relate to the discussion topic. You will want to have a sign-in sheet so you know who attended. Ask attendees to sit with others they do not know, and ask for a volunteer from each table to act as the facilitator. The facilitator will keep the conversation on track by limiting sidebar discussions and should take notes summarizing the conversation; you also could have separate facilitators and note takers.

Begin the meeting with a short welcome where you explain how you selected the discussion topic, why it is critical for the long-term success of youth with disabilities, and your efforts in this area so far. Then, explain the directions for a community conversation: participants will discuss the topic for 20 minutes; at the end of this time, they will switch to a new table where they again don't know anyone. Repeat the rotation at least three times.

Here are some questions your community conversation might use to generate discussion:

- What can we as a community do to better prepare all of our students for a successful life after high school?
- What can we do to more fully include students with disabilities in the life and activities of our high school, in both classes and extracurricular activities?
- What can we do to engage all youth more meaningfully in volunteer and civic experiences throughout our community?
- What can we do to help make high school a more engaging experience for all students?
- What can we as a community do to better support collaboration between parents and educators?
- How can we as a community better support our high school's goals of rigor, relevance, and relationships?
- How can we as a high school more fully realize our mission of _____?

During the 20-minute discussions, the table facilitator or note taker writes down important and promising ideas, resources, approaches, and any group conclusions. When the final rotation is complete, facilitators should summarize the sessions without repeating. Following the session, compile the different sets of session notes in a single, summarizing document. This should be provided to all participants via e-mail or mail.

One community transition team we know hosted a community conversation and invited representatives from agencies and businesses as well as parents and students. Their question was "How can agencies, educators, employers, and families work together to improve postschool outcomes?" The conversation yielded a diverse array of responses. After gathering participants' notes, the team organized all of the various pieces of the conversation into themes:

- *Start transition early*. The community felt that it was important to start working on postsecondary transition at a young age, and recognized that there are certain pivotal times to do this—especially in the move from middle to high school. They suggested developing intake forms in schools and working with local organizations to offer volunteer experiences for middle school students. Parents also felt that it was important for them to be educated about transition before their students entered high school.
- *Increase community collaboration*. Gathering such a diverse range of community members in one place highlighted how infrequently these individuals collaborated with each other. Community members discussed the need to establish and maintain relationships between agencies, businesses, and organizations. They brainstormed how to develop a network with businesses and community organizations and how to increase communication between schools and agencies.
- *Expand opportunities for students*. Many of the attendees recognized the need to offer students more experiences in employment and more exposure to options for postsecondary education. They also noted a need to increase the availability of housing options for students with disabilities. Building on the idea of business networks, community members developed the idea of organizing "job clubs" for students, which would meet after school to tour local businesses, write and edit resumes, and support students in developing job skills.

Conclusion

This chapter's strategies built on the personal collaboration skills discussed in Chapter 2 and discussed the value of establishing a community transition team. Through these strategies, you should be able to create your own community transition team and get the basic structure set up. The following chapters discuss how to focus and deepen your efforts once your team is up and running, and ways to maintain and sustain your endeavor.

Chapter 4

Becoming a High-Functioning Community Transition Team

Have you ever been a member of a team where you dreaded attending the meetings because nothing much happened and you felt there was little to show for your time? Where one or two people dominated the conversation and determined group actions? Where you would leave feeling like nothing had been accomplished except minimal networking? If so, this is not surprising. At certain points in our careers, we may find ourselves members of poorly functioning teams. Although many schools and communities claim to have community transition teams, upon closer examination you might find that some teams are barely functioning; their meetings are not productive, and their membership does not increase.

There are ways to create and sustain a high-functioning community transition team. Like any good relationship, teams require ongoing care and attention, and at times they must move toward uncomfortable situations rather than away. To assist you in focusing and deepening your efforts, this chapter presents four strategies:

- Strategy 17: Build Team Structure
- Strategy 18: Develop Action-Oriented Teaming
- Strategy 19: Come to Consensus
- Strategy 20: Assess Shared Leadership

Strategy 17: Build Team Structure

Whereas some community transition teams stay in existence for several years and accomplish numerous feats with highly engaged members, others fizzle out after one or two projects. Upon closer examination, it is clear that teams that thrive have certain characteristics and attributes—mostly concerning their structure and function, and including areas such as building team structure, action planning, productive decision making, and action planning.

Activity 17.1: Examine Your Team's Strengths and Weaknesses

To assist teams as they develop and sustain a strong team structure, The Community Transition Team Process Checklist (Noonan, 2011; see Appendix, Tool #5; Figure 4.1) provides a tool for self-assessment. It has been used by over 30 teams, and is designed to be used as needed several times a year to ensure that the team is on the right track for success. The checklist includes an area for teams to make notes or identify action items for immediate consideration and implementation.

For example, one community transition team was doing well but rarely reviewed any data. After completing the Process Checklist, the team noted this lack as an action item. At the following meeting, a team member from the local chamber of commerce brought employment data and an educator who provided transition services shared postschool outcomes data related to employment. The team's discussion resulted in an increased effort to partner with local employers to create summer work opportunities.

Members of another community transition team realized, after completing the Process Checklist, that they were not sharing team activities and progress with school administration. The resulting effort culminated in a presentation to the school board and expansion of an in-school work program.

The checklist can be a valuable tool for your team, as well. By completing the checklist, you can get an idea of which items need further attention, brainstorm items for an action plan, and celebrate your successes. Typically, teams are considered successful if they answer "yes" to at least 80% of these items (though of course the goal is always for 100% affirmative answers). As with all tools, a blank form for your use can be found in Appendix, Tool #5.

Activity 17.2: Complete the Team Functioning Scale

How do we determine if our team is having good meetings? To enact sustainable improvements, community transition team meetings must be structured, focused, and supportive of meaningful communication and shared decision making. To better understand overall team functioning, you can use the Team Functioning Scale (Gaumer Erickson & Noonan, 2012; see Appendix, Tool #6). This tool provides observable, concrete examples of poor team functioning as well as of excellent team functioning. The process assists teams in self-correcting to become as productive as possible, thereby retaining and better engaging membership.

The Team Functioning Scale

- Evaluates overall functioning of community transition team meetings.
- Indicates how team members observe team functioning around the subdomains of structure, communication, and focus.
- Is quick and easy to complete.
- Supports continual improvement in the quality and functioning of meetings by identifying key areas for improvement.

Figure 4.1

The Community Transition Team Process Checklist

	Left	Rating	Right
Structure	Meeting roles unassigned	1 2 3 ④ 5	Multiple meeting roles assigned prior to the meeting (e.g.. facilitator, note-taker)
	Ever-changing start and stop times (e.g., members straggle in, waiting for leadership. meetings sometimes cancelled)	1 ② 3 4 5	Meeting starts and ends on time as scheduled
	Irregular attendance by team members	1 2 3 ④ 5	Nearly all team members attend
	Nonexistent or limited use of meeting minutes/notes	1 2 3 ④ 5	Agenda developed and available prior to meetings
	Nonexistent or limited use of meeting minutes/notes	1 2 3 4 ⑤	Minutes/notes taken during meeting and distributed to all team members alter the meeting
Communication	Minimal team member engagement (e.g., members off-task. distracted)	1 ② 3 4 5	High level of engagement from all team members (e.g., verbal input, attention, willingness to complete tasks)
	Discussions disjointed (e.g., numerous interruptions, sidebar conversations)	1 ② 3 4 5	Discussions stay on track; no sidebar conversations
	Poor team member communication (e.g., aggressive tones, lack of listening, disrespect)	1 2 ③ 4 5	Team members communicate effectively (e.g., speak directly, ask questions. express support, restate ideas)
	Disagreements/conflicts aren't addressed (e.g., disgruntled team members. talking behind backs)	1 2 ③ 4 5	Disagreements/conflicts are addressed (e.g., problem solving, respect, listening)
	Some members are not valued as important to the team	1 ② 3 4 5	Members value each other's roles and contributions
	Members are not provided time/forum to share viewpoints; limited discussion time before a decision is made	1 ② 3 4 5	All viewpoints shared and given adequate time prior to decision-making (e.g., discussion of options and consequences)
	Final decision made with limited input by team (e.g., one person makes decision. limited influence, no voting)	1 2 ③ 4 5	Shared decision-making with balanced intluence of team members (e.g., voting on decisions. discussion of options)
Focus	Lack of meeting purpose (e.g., meeting "lor the sake or meeting")	1 2 3 4 ⑤	Meeting has clear purpose, which is communicated in advance
	Data docs not drive decision-making	1 2 3 ④ 5	Data drives decision-making (i.e., relevant data is reviewed and discussed; decisions clearly inlluenced by data)
	No reference to past goals/action items	1 2 3 4 ⑤	Status of action items from last meeting is reviewed
	Action items not identified, unclear responsibilities	1 2 3 ④ 5	Clear action items (e.g., deadlines, person responsible)
	Meetings are not productive and do not result in progress	1 2 ③ 4 5	Meetings are productive; continual progress focused on purpose

The Team Functioning Scale (Gaumer Erickson & Noonan, 2012) should be administered individually and confidentially, to give team members an opportunity to express their true feelings about the overall functioning of the team. You are less interested in individual members' pet peeves than in aggregate results. You can administer the survey at the end of a meeting, and have members drop them in a box as they exit; other options include e-mailing the survey to all members as an attached document, or using an online survey tool such as SurveyMonkey. Ask that they complete and return to you. Be sure to tell team members that all responses are confidential and will be aggregated in reporting. Set a deadline for completion to give yourself a window to prepare the results. Then, when you have the returned surveys, average the team's scores and share the results at a team meeting (see example, Figure 4.2). When you present your report, stress that it is not expected that transition teams will have high levels of functioning across all items. Instead, the results should be used to identify strengths and prioritize areas of improvement. Note the number of responses received, and discuss whether this is representative of your membership. Celebrate successes, and discuss the processes that are in place to support areas where the team functions well. Then, prioritize needs: Which items or areas of team functioning need improvement? How could these components of team functioning be improved over the next two meetings? Also, use the results to assess the team meeting structure for the rest of the year, and beyond. What strategies might you implement to improve team functioning in the long term?

Guided discussion questions for transition teams:

- Quickly glance through the data. What are your first impressions?
- Does the number of survey participants adequately represent our team?
- Celebrate successes: Which items or areas of team functioning are going well? What processes are in place to support these high levels of functioning?
- Prioritize needs: Which items or areas of team functioning need improvement? How could these components of team functioning could be improved over the next two meetings?
- Next steps: How should the results influence our team meeting structure for the next year? What strategies can we implement to improve our team functioning in the long term?

By completing this survey, team members have an opportunity to confidentially express their feelings about overall team functioning. Furthermore, this process will assist teams in self-correcting to become as productive as possible, thereby retaining and better engaging membership. Ask your members to complete the survey while considering your last three community transition team meetings. Items on the left are examples of low team functioning, and corresponding items on the right represent high team functioning. Complete the sliding scale (1-5) between the items to relate your observed level of team functioning for your team. A completed example is shown in Figure 4.2. As with all tools in this book, a blank form for your use can be found in the Appendix, Tool #6.

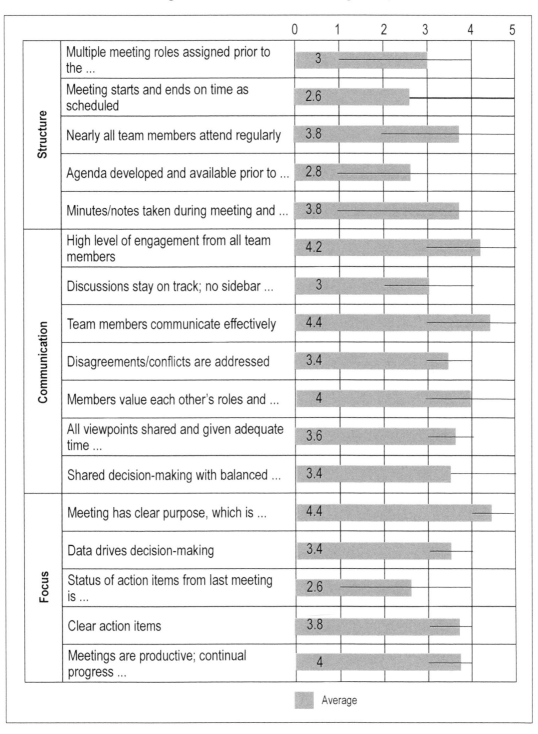

Figure 4.2
Average Scores for Team Functioning Survey

		0	1	2	3	4	5
Structure	Multiple meeting roles assigned prior to the ...	3					
	Meeting starts and ends on time as scheduled	2.6					
	Nearly all team members attend regularly	3.8					
	Agenda developed and available prior to ...	2.8					
	Minutes/notes taken during meeting and ...	3.8					
Communication	High level of engagement from all team members	4.2					
	Discussions stay on track; no sidebar ...	3					
	Team members communicate effectively	4.4					
	Disagreements/conflicts are addressed	3.4					
	Members value each other's roles and ...	4					
	All viewpoints shared and given adequate time ...	3.6					
	Shared decision-making with balanced ...	3.4					
Focus	Meeting has clear purpose, which is ...	4.4					
	Data drives decision-making	3.4					
	Status of action items from last meeting is ...	2.6					
	Clear action items	3.8					
	Meetings are productive; continual progress ...	4					

▨ Average

Note. Reprinted with permission from Team Functioning Scale, by A. Gaumer Erickson & P. Noonan. Copyright 2012 by the Center for Research on Learning, University of Kansas.

After all members have submitted their checklists or you have reached your submission deadline, you should try to organize the data in a meaningful way. A report with visuals (e.g., charts and graphs) makes it easy to quickly see which items and domains are strengths and areas of difficulty for your team.

EXAMPLE: Team Functioning Survey from Oregon School

Nine people on a community transition team in Oregon completed the Team Functioning Survey and then determined their combined results. They discussed the results and were proud that there is a high level of engagement of team members and effective communication. However, they realized that as a team, they were failing to honor start and stop times and didn't followup on past action steps, both of which were negatively impacting attendance. They decided to make these two items a priority for upcoming meetings.

Strategy 18: Develop Action-Oriented Teaming

The most effective community transition teams tend to be action-oriented, meaning the members come together not just to share updates and network, but also with a shared purpose. Action-oriented team members work together on a continual basis to carry out activities that are broken down into tasks.

Becoming an action-oriented team requires team planning, where team members have multiple, ongoing interactions to communicate ideas, listen to each other, and determine commonalities. An equitable community transition team focuses on:

- Using members' strengths and capabilities.
- Utilizing the contributions and resources of its members.
- Tapping into members' depth of knowledge about central issues.
- Following effective operational procedures.
- Being competent in diverse issues.
- Creating an effective networking system.
- Communicating openly.
- Sharing responsibility (Stodden, Brown, Galloway, Mrazek, & Noy, 2005, p. 15)

It can be difficult to build in time and structure for this level of planning. In order to develop a dynamic and effective process for community transition team planning, you will need to recognize the importance of developing formal and informal relationships with key community members by using a flexible and creative process that meets the needs of individual communities. One way to accomplish this is to work as a group to determine periods of time that can be dedicated to planning. Ideally, identify a neutral, private meeting space where members can feel comfortable expressing opinions. Make certain that all members can attend (you might explore using free online meeting planning tools such as Doodle, Meet-o-Matic, or Schedule Once).

To create an effective action plan, the first step for community transition teams is to *clarify*. Make sure that all team members understand the purpose of the planning process, to avoid confusion and conflicting roles. Having a clear purpose grounded in the team's shared vision will help keep the process focused and allow the team to accomplish its goals. For example, one team clarified the purpose of their planning process by agreeing to a 4-hour meeting where they would reflect on the previous year's accomplishments, review outcomes data from members, identify areas of need, and create an action plan for the next 12 months.

Throughout the action-planning process, it is important to ensure that each individual on the team demonstrates shared participation and responsibility

during the decision-making process. This can occur through a variety of collaborative processes including consensus-building and team agreement strategies. It is essential that team members share ownership for decisions, assume responsibility for results, and maintain individual integrity. Like any team, community transition teams gain when the relationships among members add value to the efforts of the team as a whole: team members can collectively create visions, ideas, goals, and solutions that are not likely to occur when they work in isolation.

Activity 18.1: Create an Action Plan

An action plan is not simply a detailed task list; but it's actually a more involved process. In essence, an action plan is a fluid document that helps to define goals, break the goals down into activities, and assign steps to team members with dates. The process of creating an action plan is multistaged and promotes transparency and accountability. To create an action plan, here are the summarized steps:

Step 1: Discuss and clarify your community's areas of need.
Step 2: Clarify and prioritize goals.
Step 3: Brainstorm potential activities/strategies that will help you reach your goals.
Step 4: Flesh out and finalize action plan.
Step 5: Follow-up.

In the following paragraphs, each step will be expanded upon to provide detailed directions so that your team can complete the action planning process.

Step 1: Discuss and clarify your community's areas of need. Before beginning action planning, discuss the accomplishments of the team in the past 6 months, past year, and since its development. Reflect on changes in membership, accomplishment of activities, and the overall effect of your work. Ask each member to relate examples of how the transition team's work has furthered its goals to improve outcomes for people with disabilities. (Be sure to acknowledge individual members' contribution and work.)

Next, review your written mission statement. Discuss the intent of the statement so that all team members have a joint understanding of the purpose of the teamwork. If major membership changes have occurred, you may find it necessary to return to Strategy 12 (see Chapter 3) to redevelop your shared vision. Remember, the action planning process is for the sole purpose of working towards the shared vision, and that vision should be considered throughout.

Finally, identify the current, most pressing needs of students and adults with disabilities in the community by having team members vote on which areas of need they would like to address in the coming year. Use several large pieces of notepad paper. As a group, generate one large list of needs, being sure to include perspectives from all members. After the discussion, give each person five votes of descending weights (e.g., 5, 4, 3, 2, 1). All members vote on the most important areas of need to address in the coming year. Table 4.1 provides an example from a state-level transition team. In this example, the top four areas of need received many more votes than other areas; although all areas of need are important, dramatic differences in the number of votes will help you prioritize the most pressing issues facing your team.

Step 2: Clarify and prioritize goals. Understanding the goals and priorities of your community transition team is an important step when forming partnerships. Step 1's needs assessment will help determine which goals your team needs to address. There are many different things to take into account when writing your team's goals. Highly prioritized areas of need are a good place to start, but your team also needs to consider its shared vision, the feasibility of accomplishing various goals, and the resources available.

After you have identified several goals (at least two, and at most five), reread your team's mission statement and reconsider current community needs. Then, as a group, discuss:

- Costs/benefits in terms of money, time, and resources for each of the potential goals.
- How accomplishing the goals would support youth with disabilities and the outcomes of adults with disabilities (e.g., working, living independently, higher education/training).
- Overall value accomplishing each goal would add to the community.

Table 4.1
Sample Rank Ordering of Identified Community Needs

NEED IN COMMUNITY	NUMBER OF VOTES
Agencies do NOT share information data with each other	25
Educators don't get "transition," have no idea what to do	17
Lack of data on people with disabilities	16
Lack of collaboration within school between SPED/GenEd/School counselor	15
Lack of knowledge of other agencies (no referral)	12
Certain students don't get access to appropriate vocational programs	12
Lack of self-determination skills	9
Difficult to share info	9
Lack of self-advocacy for children	7
Postsecondary education failure	5
Prerequisite college coursework	4
Forms of eligibility can be barriers	3
Some career centers and vocational programs exclude students with disabilities, assessed out	3
Lack of individual planning for all kids	3
Staff have too large caseloads	3
Vocational education vs. academics ➤ policies are fractured	3
Parent denial (family not wanting to talk about future, fear of unknown)	2
Rural areas, poverty, family pressures	2
Lack of school/family communication	2
Transition not a part of daily high school	2
The structure of staff roles	1
Prerequisite college coursework	1
Recidivism (GED vs. diploma)	1

Next, discuss challenges your team could face in the upcoming year by answering the following questions:

- What challenges do you think our Community Transition Team will face in the next 6 months, 12 months, and long-term?
- How could the identified goals respond to these challenges?

If the goals do not seem to address the challenges, discuss how they could be changed to respond to potential challenges.

Although the top-ranked area of need may seem very pressing, you might determine that it does not fit well with your shared vision or that your community transition team has not yet built up needed resources. Once you have narrowed down your goals, write them down in language that is clear and easy to understand. Make sure that each team member understands the intention of the goals.

Finally, review the list of goals in light of any challenges the team has encountered and the value that you provide or would like to provide to the community. Which goals should you focus on first? Which can be advanced through collaboration? Rank the goals from highest to lowest (see sample worksheet, Figure 4.3).

Step 3: Brainstorm potential activities and strategies that will help you reach your goals. Purposive brainstorming done in a structured way is a good way to generate potential solutions and activities. There are several key steps in hosting a brainstorming session with a large group.

The most important part of brainstorming is to capture everyone's ideas and allow each person to express an idea. Having a facilitator helps ensure the success of a brainstorming session. The facilitator should be in charge of displaying the group's work (e.g., on large sheets of paper using markers, or a projector linked to a computer). Begin by agreeing on the amount of time that will be spent brainstorming. Depending on the size of the group, many brainstorming sessions last 20 to 30 minutes. Note that many ideas come from building from others' ideas. State the amount of time for the activity and then adhere to the time limitation.

Next, state the purpose and some ground rules for the activity. One example of a purpose is "the purpose of this brainstorming session is to generate ideas about increasing parent involvement in school activities." Share ground rules as well, such as: (a) be positive, (b) do not discuss implementing the ideas during this time, and (c) use active listening and restate ideas for clarification.

The facilitator will pay close attention as individuals provide ideas and input, and will notice if any participants are not engaged in the activity. It is important to encourage participation and input from all attendees. Then, the facilitator will read each idea and allow time for discussion and clarification. Note, new ideas will emerge and can be added at this time. The activity should conclude on time with a large list of potential solutions and possible activities.

Figure 4.3
Prioritized Goals Work Sheet

List and briefly describe your prioritized goals.

Goal 1:

Goal 2:

Goal 3:

After you've reached your time limit, participants should vote toward what they think are the best ideas. You can limit the number of votes participants are allowed, or ask them to rank their top five to seven favorite ideas.

Determine a set of criteria for judging. Then, discuss which ideas scored the highest and determine what will best help your team achieve its goals.

For novice transition teams, goals and activities should be easily accomplished so that the team can enjoy and recognize early success. (As teams begin to accomplish work together, celebrate early successes to build trust and team commitment.) Table 4.2 provides some examples of community transition team goals, and activities groups have identified to undertake. Once you have identified and rank ordered your top five goals, and activities that might help you achieve each, you can turn these ideas into an action plan.

Step 4: Flesh out and finalize action plan. Your action plan is based on the goals you identified in Step 2 and the activities and strategies for each goal from Step 3. The Action Plan Form (see Appendix, Tool #7) provides a template for organizing this information, and also serves as a progress monitoring tool. As with all documents you create for the team, the action plan should include your mission statement; this will help focus the team on ensuring that all goals and activities relate to the team's overall vision. Activities should be described with as much detail as possible so that anyone who reads the action plan can understand the scope of work; it helps to use bullets and limit acronyms. Similarly, specifically identify individuals (by name) who are responsible for each activity; avoid using vague terms (e.g., team or school folks). Also, make sure that workloads are evenly distributed among team members. For relatively long-term activities (e.g., host transition fair in spring), identify subactivities with interim due dates. It is necessary, although at times difficult, to identify outcomes in advance of the work; however, identifying outcomes clarifies both individual responsibilities and team expectations. Begin all subsequent meetings with an update on the action plan activities; ensure that all team members are aware of the current status of each project and progress accomplishing the activity. Figure 4.4 illustrates how Tool #7 can be used to both develop and monitor your action plan.

For "What's the Outcome?," identify at least one outcome for each activity. For example, "Three new employers agree to allow job-shadowing." In Figure 4.4, you can find a sample action plan to give you an idea of how the form should look when you are finished.

Step 5: Follow up. Action plans are a very helpful tool, but only if everyone can access them. Be sure to disseminate them widely and update often. Many teams keep their action plans on Google Drive or other shared online spaces to ensure all members have access to up-to-date information.

Action plans are fluid and ever changing, and although it's tempting to leave completed activities on the action plan, be sure to delete them or mark as done. This will enable the team to visualize progress, which helps team members feel like they belong to a functioning team that's worth their time.

Finally, at every meeting, be sure to review whether action steps were completed. If not, discuss any barriers to action plan items and potential solutions, and address steps that have not been completed by the due date. Acknowledge those who worked hard and document your successes. Figure 4.5 shows one community transition team's reflection on the action plan items they completed during one year. As you can see, they set a total of five goals, all of which they met. The team provides additional information about goals when necessary.

> ### Roadblock Alert 2
>
> Although it's tempting to concentrate activities in response to the highest ranked need, it may not be the most practical one to address. For example, one team identified a need for more data sharing among agencies; however, they grew to realize that activities or improvement in this area fell more to state leadership and administrators. The group was powerless. To prevent this, be sure that you choose topics and activities that are easily accomplished by the group that will certainly have an effect.

Once you have completed the action plan and followed through on your items, you deserve to celebrate your team's accomplishments. The amount of work a community transition team can accomplish over the span of a single year is truly amazing.

Table 4.2

Sample Community Transition Team Goals and Activities

GOALS	ACTIVITIES
• Increase student self-determination • Increase student involvement in community employment • Increase parent participation • Increase agency involvement • Increase opportunities for stakeholders to be involved in transition • Educate businesses, community members, school personnel, families, and students about how people with disabilities can be productive members of the community • Develop mentoring relationships • Build more community/business partnerships	• Create a resource directory and transition brochures • Create a community transition team web site • Develop training workshops • Develop parent communication tools • Survey businesses' and students' expectations of work experiences • Add transition information to district web site • Develop listing of community services and support agencies (resource directory/searchable web site) • Host a transition fair for parents and students (include general ed students) • Develop school/business internships • Recruit more diverse team members (retirees, juvenile justice, mental health) • Reorganize community transition team as a nonprofit and apply for funding • Develop business partnerships through open houses, attending Chamber of Commerce meetings, joining civic groups • Develop student-run transition group to inform activities • Create a comprehensive graduation guide for students • Create and implement a career program for students with significant disabilities • Develop a comprehensive list of potential employers and agencies that can be utilized for employment and training opportunities • Create a packet of transition information for students at the middle school level • Provide employers with more information about transitioning students • Establish a subcommittee focused on barriers to student employment • Develop a freshman transition night

Figure 4.4
Sample Action Plan

School District(s): Sample City

Team Leader: Mary Jo & Laura

Team Name: Sample County Community Transition Team

Vision: The purpose of the Sample County Community Transition Team is to motivate and empower our youth by introducing outside resources and providing multiple opportunities for meaningful areas of employment.

GOAL 1: Educate the community about the Sample County Community Transition Team.
What needs to take place within the next 1-6 months?

STEPS	WHO	BY WHEN	WHAT'S THE OUTCOME?	STATUS UPDATES: DATE: MET/ NOT MET
1. Create a brochure – Student driven	Jackie	10/16/12	Brochure completed and mailed to local businesses. Student created	Met
2. Send invitation letters and follow-up phone calls to all invited to meeting	Hadley and Kimi	Letters – 10/19/12 Phone calls-10/26/12	Letters mailed	Met
3. Secure location for meeting and order lunch	Sarah	10/16/12	Meeting scheduled at local church. Lunch will be catered	Met
4. CTT information meeting for community representatives	Josh	11/2/12 10am-12pm	17 local and community members present at the meeting	Met
5. Schedule monthly team meetings	Sarah	11/02/12	Date was scheduled for January. Meeting will be in Blue City.	Met

Figure 4.4
Sample Action Plan *(cont'd)*

GOAL 2: Increase workplace experiences for our students
What needs to take place within the next 1-6 months?

STEPS	WHO	BY WHEN	WHAT'S THE OUTCOME?	STATUS UPDATES: DATE: MET/ NOT MET
1. Create a resource list from all members present	Andrea, Hadley, Kimi, and Sarah	12/31/12	List was created on chart paper during local CTT	Met
2. Brainstorm ideas of possible workplace job options	CTT members at local meeting	11/02/12	Several jobs were discussed and listed. Local agencies were excited about possible work experiences for students.	Met

GOAL 3: Collaborate with local businesses and agencies to create work experiences for students during the 2013-2014 school year.
What needs to take place within the next 1-6 months?

STEPS	WHO	BY WHEN	WHAT'S THE OUTCOME?	STATUS UPDATES: DATE: MET/ NOT MET
1. Contact school to work – Vocational Technology	Shay	12/2012	Developing potential jobs and job skills with classroom instruction	Met
2. Approach potential employers for the 2013-2014 school year	Jackie, Andrea, and Ed	May 2013	Work experience to develop Emotional Quotient & Intelligence Quotient skills.	Met

Figure 4.5
Reflection on Completed Action Items

Kirksville CTT—Team TEACH

What we have done:

✓Developed an introduction letter to recruit other members.

✓Delivered introduction letter to 26 potential members.

- Adult employment agencies
- Workforce Development
- GAMM
- Disability office at Truman Stete University
- Juvenile Justice Center
- Drug/Alcohol treatment facility
- Small business owners
- Mark Twain Behavioral Health
- Kirksville Area Technical Center
- Middle school special education teachers
- Parents of middle school and high school students and graduates
- Social Security Office
- YMCA/Parks and Recreation
- Chamber of commerce
- Children's Divlsion

✓ Scheduled a large group meeting for January 19, 2010

✓ Reviewed books from Full Life Ahead (student/family guide to planning)

✓ Decided to make tabbed three ring binders for parents, students, and teachers to check out to show what transition agencies are in Kirksville.

- Nine tabs to include
  - Education
  - Employment
  - Housing
  - Legal (including guardianship options)
  - Financial Help
  - Healthcare
  - Social/Recreation/Leisure
  - Transportation
  - Miscellaneous

Strategy 19: Come to Consensus

Consensus building can be a long and difficult process. Luckily, there are many strategies to speed up the consensus-building process.

Activity 19.1: The Five-Finger Vote

The five-finger vote (Golden & Gall, 2000) is a great way to make sure your team members are able to recognize their level of consensus and take action appropriately. This strategy can help you avoid long, unnecessary discussions when consensus already exists, and it can show you when to schedule for a more efficient use of time when members disagree.

The five-finger vote is a quick and easy way to gauge a group's feelings on an issue. At any point during the meeting, any member can ask for the team's feelings on a topic. To get an immediate assessment, each member raises his or her hand while showing a number of fingers that expresses his or her opinion. Members respond by raising their hands with a certain number of fingers (i.e., zero = If zero fingers are raised, that indicates that the team member dislikes the proposed idea or is strongly opposed to it. If all five fingers are raised, that member indicates his or her agreement and support for full adoption of the measure.) Don't stop to tally up each member's finger count – you are looking for large trends within the group, not a detailed vote. After you've scanned the responses, you can quickly assess and plan your next steps. If the group has a very positive reaction, you can agree to approve the item and move on. If the group's reaction is very negative or there is lots of disagreement, you can schedule a time for future in-depth discussion of the issue.

The five-finger vote is a great way to make sure your team members are able to recognize their level of consensus and take action appropriately. This strategy can help you avoid long, unnecessary discussions when consensus already exists, and it can show you when to schedule for a more efficient use of time when members disagree.

Your group can use this strategy for more than just determining action items. The five-finger vote also can be used to decide whether take a break or push through and finish the meeting earlier. You can ask members for their feelings on the issue. If some members have strong opinions, this strategy allows voting to reflect those opinions far more accurately than a normal vote.

Another use of the five-finger vote is for general meeting assessment. At the end of each meeting, ask members to reflect on the meeting's value (i.e., zero = meeting was not useful at all; 5 = very productive). If the meeting receives positive reviews, the vote will prompt members to reflect on the value of the time spent in the meeting, which can in turn promote future attendance. On the other hand, if members feel dissatisfied, you may engage in a short conversation about how to improve future meetings.

This activity makes consensus building quick and simple by encouraging immediate feedback and results. When team members see how their opinions directly influence the meeting's course, they feel empowered and are more inclined to participate.

Strategy 20: Assess Shared Leadership

To make sure that your team is employing principles of shared leadership (see Chapter 3, Strategy 14), you should periodically assess the level of shared leadership in your transition team. The goal of this type of assessment is to get an idea of the group's overall use of shared leadership principles; the process should identify whether members share the same vision and commitment to the team's mission. It also provides a guide to individual perceptions among team members. No one person can truly determine the level of shared leadership; whereas one team member may feel that leadership responsibilities are appropriately distributed, another may feel excluded or overburdened. For more information on organizing your team using shared leadership, check out Strategy 14: Organizing your community transition team.

Activity 20.1: Complete the Shared Leadership Survey

To more accurately assess the level of shared leadership in your group, administer the Shared Leadership Survey (see Appendix, Tool #8) to all group members. This survey is intended to reflect both individual team members' impressions of the distribution of responsibility and provide an overall reflection of how effectively your team is working. Figure 4.6 is a sample of a completed survey. It includes the domain names for each item, whereas the tool included in the Appendix does not. Administering a "blind" survey (i.e., without domain names) may provide more unbiased responses from your team members.

Averaging individual results by item and by domain will give you an understanding of the group's overall use of shared leadership principles. The example above shows a sample filled-out survey from one group member. This member's responses turned out to be very representative of her group's overall trends. Below, you can see Figure 4.7 is a chart showing our example group's overall averages by domain an example summarizing results from the Shared Leadership Survey. This particular team had high average scores for collaboration, culture, and delegation, but the Vision domain had a much lower average. From these results, our sample group spurred into action. Upon seeing the results of this survey, they realized that though their team had developed a shared vision when first formed, some members had left, and a lot of new members had joined. They had not redeveloped or explained their shared vision statement to incoming members. This team decided that member turnover was substantial enough that it needed to start from scratch and redevelop its vision, one that was representative for all members.

Figure 4.6
Completed Shared Leadership Survey

DOMAIN	ITEM	SCORE (1=STRONGLY DISAGREE, 3=NEUTRAL, 5=STRONGLY AGREE)				
Collaboration	I collaborate regularly with my team members to achieve goals.	1	2	3	④	5
Vision	My team has a shared vision with agreed-upon goals.	1	②	3	4	5
Delegation	The formal leaders in my team are willing to delegate some control to informal leaders.	1	2	3	4	⑤
Culture	Our team members trust each other to work effectively and get the job done.	1	2	3	④	5
Vision	I understand my team's purpose and goals.	1	2	③	4	5
Delegation	When major decisions must be made, team members are involved in the decision process in a meaningful way.	1	2	3	④	5
Culture	Each team member's unique expertise is valued and utilized.	1	2	3	④	5
Culture	When I think of leadership, I think of a shared mission to learn and construct knowledge collaboratively.	1	2	3	4	⑤
Collaboration	I have an excellent rapport with at least two other team members.	1	2	3	4	⑤
Delegation	When a new task arises, leadership responsibilities are determined by members' strengths, not by formal titles.	1	2	3	④	5
Culture	I feel confident taking on leadership responsibilities in this team.	1	2	3	④	5
Delegation	If the team's chairperson left, the team would continue to make progress toward its goals.	1	2	3	4	⑤
Vision	When team members work together as leaders, they share beliefs, values, and goals.	①	2	3	4	5
Delegation	As a leader in the team, I have responsibilities in multiple roles/positions.	1	2	3	④	5
Culture	All members of my team value collective efficacy.	1	2	3	4	⑤
Collaboration	I know what strengths and skills each of the other team members possess.	1	2	3	④	5
Collaboration	In addition to the team's formally designated leaders, I can identify at least two other team members who act as informal leaders.	1	2	3	4	⑤
Vision	The leadership roles available in my group result from the needs arising from our goals.	1	2	③	4	5
Collaboration	I feel that every other team member has a capacity for leadership.	1	2	③	4	5
Delegation	Multiple people are trusted with information and decision-making for every activity our group undertakes.	1	2	3	④	5

Note. Reprinted with permission from Shared Leadership Measure, by J. A. Brussow, 2013, Lawrence, KS: Center for Research on Learning, University of Kansas. Copyright 2013 by the Center for Research on Learning, University of Kansas.

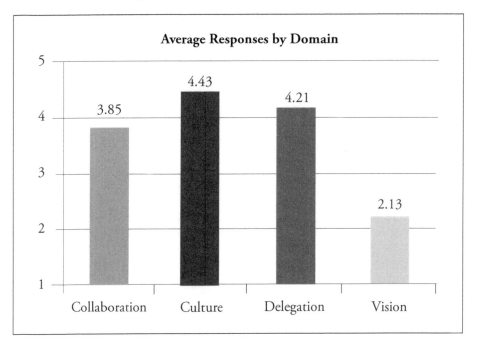

Figure 4.7
Sample Results of Shared Leadership Survey

Conclusion

The intent of this chapter is to help you increase your team's levels of internal collaboration, productivity, and achievement. If at any point in your team's life span you feel the team's focus or morale starting to dwindle, don't hesitate to return to these strategies. Each of these can be used repeatedly throughout a team's development.

Chapter 5 discusses how to use data as a team. Believe it or not, you have actually already started to use data – Activity 20.1, The Shared Leadership Survey. is one example of data collection and use; there are ways to use other types of data to help your team.

Chapter 5

Using Data to Inform Decision Making

With Madeline Wetta

In this time of increased accountability, data-based decision making is a critical component of school improvement. Over the past decade, teachers, principals, and other school professionals have become more aware of the importance of data collection, data analysis, and data-based decision making. Data-based decision making is "a process in which school personnel engage in ongoing analysis of data from multiple sources to provide a comprehensive picture of a school's strengths and challenges and develop a plan to prioritize and address challenges" (Feldman & Tung, 2001, p. 4) This process of systematic investigation and interpretation of data helps schools evaluate their teaching practices and student achievement. Furthermore, data-based decision making is a critical component in promoting evidence-based educational interventions and building learner-centered leadership.

Transition education and services can also benefit from the data-based decision making process. It can help community transition teams better understand the strengths and needs of youth with disabilities, evaluate the services they receive, and identify areas for improvement. Using data to determine the extent to which teaching practices influence students' learning and behavior is essential to improving teachers' instructional strategies (Skalski & Romero, 2011). Transition educators can also use data gathering and analysis as a strategy to collaborate with others and create a shared understanding of purpose, facilitating positive collaboration. The following strategies are discussed in this chapter:

- Strategy 21: Use Data as a Community Transition Team
- Strategy 22: Use Data Already Available to Your Community Transition Team
- Strategy 23: Gather Information and Collect Data

Strategy 21: Use Data as a Community Transition Team

Systematic, data-based decision making helps schools implement the most effective practices and instructional strategies. Data can be used to support collaboration between educators, administrators, adult service providers, and parents; unfortunately, attaining a shared understanding of data can be difficult. Although the vast majority of educators these days would like to become "more reflective practitioners," few have the skills to perform sufficient data collection and analysis, and make decisions based on data. Even in a supportive, highly engaging school environment, efficient data use is difficult without training. Few teachers and school personnel have adequate technical support to compile, analyze and interpret data (Stringfield, Wayman, & Yakimowski, 2005).

Activity 21.1: Educate the Team on Data-Based Decision Making

Skalski & Romero (2011) noted that, for schools to implement data-based decision making, staff must understand what data relating to teaching practices is available and how to use it, schools must provide training for teachers to learn about data collection and interpretation, and professional collaboration must occur so staff can share ideas and discuss which teaching strategies can be further developed. You can follow a similar process of educating community transition team members about what data is, and how to use it, to effectively strengthen transition education and services. These steps can be modified to reflect the nature of transition, which involves a number of organizations and individuals that operate outside the school. Use the following steps to guide the use of data in your team:

Roadblock Alert 1

Often, we have lots of data available on a plethora of topics. Be sure to plan and discuss in detail what data your team needs and relate it specifically to the issues or needs you are trying to address so that your energy isn't wasted tracking down, analyzing, and explaining data that are irrelevant to your mission.

ROADBLOCK ALERT!

Identify sources of transition-related data. Some data are or may be already available to community transition teams, including postschool outcomes data, student achievement and behavioral data, and employment data. Because your team includes transition professionals, community members, and agency representatives, it will have diverse perspectives and insight into different areas. Discuss as a team what other types of data you need, and investigate sources of these data as well as means to collecting it.

Decide what data your team should investigate. This chapter relates all example data to transition. However, schools might have data that are not explicitly relevant to transition, or they might have to find sources of data outside of what is usually considered. Teams consisting of transition professionals, community members, and agency representatives will also likely organize their investigation differently than would strictly school-based data teams. Remember that members of a community transition team are likely to have insight into different areas, and investigative tasks should reflect this diversity.

Determine how data is related to transition education or services. As mentioned before, Some data can be applied explicitly to transition education and services, such as post-school outcomes data, which we will discuss below. Other data, such as that on academic achievement and disciplinary action, may not obviously relate to transition education and services, but still affects successful transition.

Team members need to learn the data. As with any team examining data, all data should be distributed to team members, and those who are most expert concerning them should offer an explanation so that understanding can be reached by all members.

Teams need to share ideas and discuss strategies about what services, curriculum, or strategies can be deployed. Each team member will have his or her own ideas about what actions to take based on the results of your data. Some members may have different interpretations or reactions than you expect, and that's fine. Data-based decision making allows members to use their unique perspectives to come up with solutions.

Strategy 22: Use Data Already Available to Your Community Transition Team

22

School districts are required to collect and report transition-specific data to the state annually and each state in turn reports its data to the federal government. These data are directly relevant to the activities of community transition teams and include postschool outcomes data, school performance data, and employment data.

Postschool outcomes data. Each state's effectiveness of transition planning and other special education indicators are evaluated through its State Performance Plan. This plan outlines the activities and targets for 20 indicators; at the school level, the State Performance Plan indicators provide a framework for evaluating the effectiveness of transition services. Of the 20 indicators included in the State Performance Plan, four are directly related to transition and influenced by interagency collaboration:

- Indicator 1: Percentage of youth with individualized education programs (IEPs) graduating from high school with a regular diploma
- Indicator 2: Percentage of youth with IEPs dropping out of high school
- Indicator 13: Percentage of youth aged 16 or above with an IEP with adequate goals and transition services

- Indicator 14: Percentage of youth who had IEPs, are no longer in secondary school and who have been competitively employed, enrolled in postsecondary school, or both within one year of leaving high school.

School performance data. District and school data can be very helpful in understanding student achievement as it relates to transition. This information can help identify trends across the general student population and call attention to populations of students in need of particular attention. Collection of academic achievement and behavioral data varies from state to state and district to district. Some examples of data that districts and schools may collect are:

- Measures of proficiency in math and English/language arts.
- Schoolwide evaluation tool results.
- Number of expulsions and suspensions.
- Disciplinary data such as office referrals.
- Literacy levels.

Employment data. Another type of publicly accessible data that can be useful for community transition teams is employment data from state departments of labor (http://www.dol.gov/dol/topic/statistics/). Individual state web sites often offer local and regional information, such as labor force data, industry employment, hours and earnings, and unemployment data by county; occupational wages and estimated employment; projections of statewide employment growth; local job vacancy surveys by occupational groups; education requirements; and wages.

Activity 22.1: Use Postschool Outcomes Data

Data from Indicator 14 can be instrumental in understanding how effective your transition education and services are in promoting high-quality adult outcomes (e.g., working, succeeding in postsecondary training/education, living independently). Postschool outcome results also can help teams form a plan for improvement and mobilize others (e.g., employers, parents, co-workers) for shared work.

Remember, local school districts are required to collect this data to submit it to the state use this knowledge when trying to track down the data. Once you have received the data, it's best to organize it into a format that other members can easily understand. In Figure 5.1, you can see an example of how one school district organized their postschool outcomes data and then used it as a springboard for action planning.

Figure 5.1 illustrates how to use data about postschool outcomes to inform planning. One community transition team used information the school district used their postschool outcomes data to increase their understanding of current program strengths and limitations, as well as to assist in setting goals for improvement. First, school staff and administrators gathered the data by contacting former students about their living, work and education 1 year following exit from high school. The data were presented both in a table and in graphs and charts.

Figure 5.1
Sample Postschool Outcomes Data Report

Sample USD PSO Story
Data reflects 2010-2011 Sample USD Exiters

Sample USD			
Eligible for survey	40		
Respondents	36		
Response Rate	90%		
	Represented	Under-represented	Over-represented
Gender			✓
Ethnicity	✓		
Exit Reason (Dropout)	✓		
Categories of Disability:	Represented	Under-represented	Over-represented
LD	✓		
ED	✓		
MR	✓		
All Others	✓		

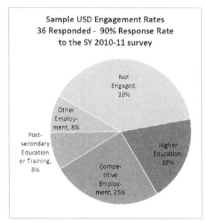

Sample USD Engagement Rates
36 Responded - 90% Response Rate
to the SY 2010-11 survey

- Not Engaged, 39%
- Higher Education, 19%
- Competitive Employment, 25%
- Post-secondary Education or Training, 8%
- Other Employment, 8%

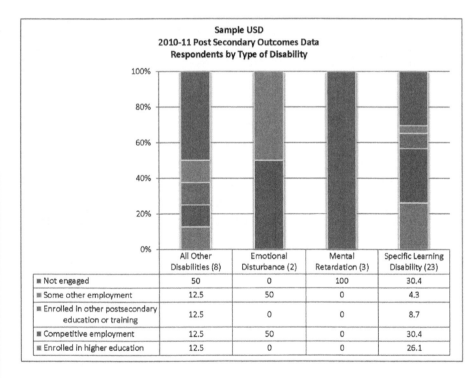

Sample USD
2010-11 Post Secondary Outcomes Data
Respondents by Type of Disability

	All Other Disabilities (8)	Emotional Disturbance (2)	Mental Retardation (3)	Specific Learning Disability (23)
▪ Not engaged	50	0	100	30.4
▪ Some other employment	12.5	50	0	4.3
▪ Enrolled in other postsecondary education or training	12.5	0	0	8.7
▪ Competitive employment	12.5	50	0	30.4
▪ Enrolled in higher education	12.5	0	0	26.1

Figure 5.1
Sample Postschool Outcomes Data Report *(cont'd)*

Sample USD PSO Story:
Response Rate and Representativeness

Sample USD 2010-2011 PSO
Response Rate by Demographic

	Overall	Disability Category				Gender	Ethnicity		Exit Reason
		LD	ED	MR	AO	Female	Minority	LEP	Dropout
Target Leaver Totals	40	26	2	4	8	24	1	0	9
Response Totals	36	23	2	3	8	24	1	0	8
Response Rate	90.00%	88.46%	100%	75.00%	100%	100%	100%	0.00%	88.89%

Representativeness

	Disability Category				Gender	Ethnicity		Exit Reason
	LD	ED	MR	AO	Female	Minority	LEP	Dropout
Target Leaver Representation	65.00%	5.00%	10.00%	20.00%	60.00%	2.50%	0.00%	22.50%
Respondent Representation	63.89%	5.56%	8.33%	22.22%	66.67%	2.78%	0.00%	22.22%
Difference	-1.11%	0.56%	-1.67%	2.22%	6.67%	0.28%	0.00%	-0.28%

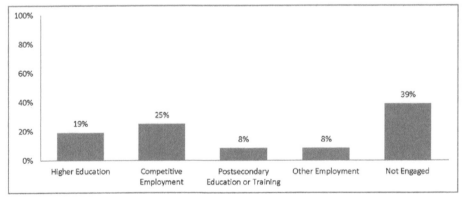

As you can see, although the district had a very high response rate (i.e., 90%), certain groups of students had a higher response rate than others. Also, the data told an alarming story: 39% of former students were not engaged, and students' rate of engagement varied dramatically between disability types, with students in certain categories performing worse than others. Continuing through the report, you will see data about response rates. These data can help you see which groups of former students your data may not be accurate for; if you have a low response rate for a group, you can't trust the results as much. The final chart shows the various types of engagement for the district's 36 graduates. Of the positive postschool outcomes, competitive employment is the most common.

After compiling the data into a report, the team considered a number of questions to help form a plan of action for improvement, including:

- What actions do we need to take to improve or maintain the current outcomes?

  Increase supports for Native American and Hispanic student populations
  Provide opportunities to students who might be interested in higher education, especially for male students

- What policies and/or procedures may be contributing to or hindering outcomes for our students?

  Emphasis on work skills, employment programs might take away from time spent promoting higher education

- What is the relationship between postschool outcomes and our graduation and/or dropout rates?

  100% of (1) dropouts are not engaged

- What further questions do we need and want to ask? What additional data do we need?

- Are there programs or interventions we can implement to improve outcomes for students with intellectual disabilities?

As a result of this discussion, The team developed a plan to begin increasing transition-aged youth's exposure to higher education options. This included asking general education faculty to help by infusing college-relevant assignments into their coursework, reaching out to university representatives to visit their high school campuses more often, and organizing campus visits for students with disabilities across the district—paying particular care in recruiting male, Native American, and Hispanic students, who might not have received the same exposure as their peers to information about postsecondary education.

Activity 22.2: Use School Performance Data

This is another type of data your schools are required to submit, so the data should be available within your district. As with PSO data, it's best to format this data into an easily-readable report once you have received it. Line charts and bar graphs are simple yet effective ways to display these data. Displaying your district's results for multiple years can help you get an idea of how achievement levels are changing through time. In Figure 5.2, we provide some example charts displaying sample math proficiency data as well as some guiding questions to help your team discuss your district's results.

These results show the sample district's math proficiency scores through time. The line chart displayed first shows the discrepancy in performance between various student groups. Clearly, math proficiency is dramatically lower for economically disadvantaged students, English language learners, and students with disabilities. These differences between groups suggest some areas of need for the example community transition team to work on.

The bottom bar graph shows math proficiency by grade level through time. As you can see from this graph, math proficiency has decreased in the 2010-11 and 2011-12 school years at the seventh and eighth grade levels, but it has increased for high school students. Why might this pattern of data occur? This would be a great question for the community transition team to tackle.

Here are some additional questions related to achievement data that your team should discuss:

- What actions do you need to take to improve or maintain the current proficiency levels in math and reading?
- What policies and/or procedures may be contributing to or hindering the improvement of your students' reading and math proficiencies?
- What other factors might be contributing to improvements/decline in certain grade levels/populations?
- How might policies and/or procedures that might be contributing to improvement for certain grade levels/populations be replicated or applied to others?
- What further questions do you need and want to ask? What other data do you need to answer those questions?

Activity 22.3: Use Employment Data

Another type of publicly accessible data that can be useful for community transition teams is employment data from Departments of Labor (http://www.dol.gov/dol/topic/statistics/). While federal information might not be particularly helpful, state Department of Labor web sites often offer local and regional information. For instance, the

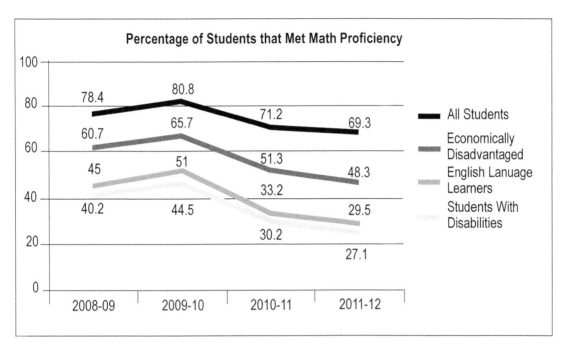

Figure 5.2
Sample School Performance Report (Math Proficiency Data)

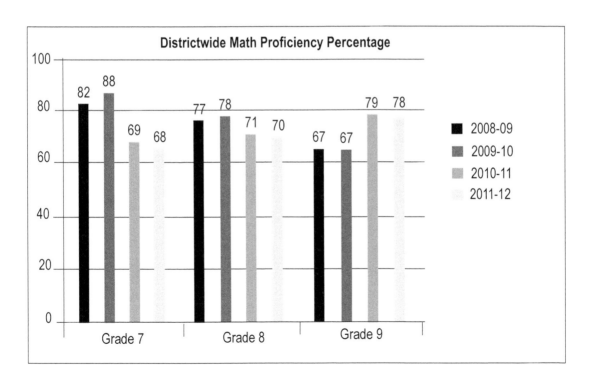

Kansas Department of Labor offers a variety of data and reports on employment both at the state level and at the local and regional level.

- A monthly labor report that includes labor force data, industry employment, hours and earnings, and unemployment data that extends to the county level http://www.dol.ks.gov/LMIS/mlr.aspx,
- A survey of Kansas workers' occupational wages and estimated employment https://klic.dol.ks.gov/gsipub/index.asp?docid=436,
- *The Kansas Occupational Outlook,* which projects statewide employment growth over a ten-year period https://klic.dol.ks.gov/gsipub/index.asp?docid=367, and
- A quarterly, local job vacancy survey that includes information about job vacancies by occupational groups, education requirements, and wages https://klic.dol.ks.gov/gsipub/index.asp?docid=437. (Kansas Department of Labor, 2013)
- All of this information can also be accessed from the Kansas Labor Information Center site: https://klic.dol.ks.gov/.

These types of employment data can be useful as your team brainstorms about expanding job experience opportunities for students in your community. These data are also useful when supporting students in their long-term transition planning (e.g., how much they would like to earn, what kind of education is necessary for certain jobs, what jobs are available in the region).

State employment data are generally presented in graphics and charts (see sample, Figure 5.3); however, if you find raw data, you will need to present the date in an easily readable format. After reviewing employment data, the transition team should consider how it applies to students in your community:

Roadblock Alert 2
Sometimes finding the data your team needs might be difficult. When organizing data-collecting or research committees, capitalize on the variety of expertise and skills of members of your group to organize data teams. Involving all members in data collection and analysis can help to make the process more efficient.

ROADBLOCK ALERT!

- What level of education do jobs available in the region require?
- Are there certain types of training students with disabilities need in order to make them more competitive for the available jobs?
- If a student has a specific goal for income level, which jobs might be suitable?
- If students relocate to a different area, how might their employment prospects change?

Figure 5.3
Sample State Employment Data

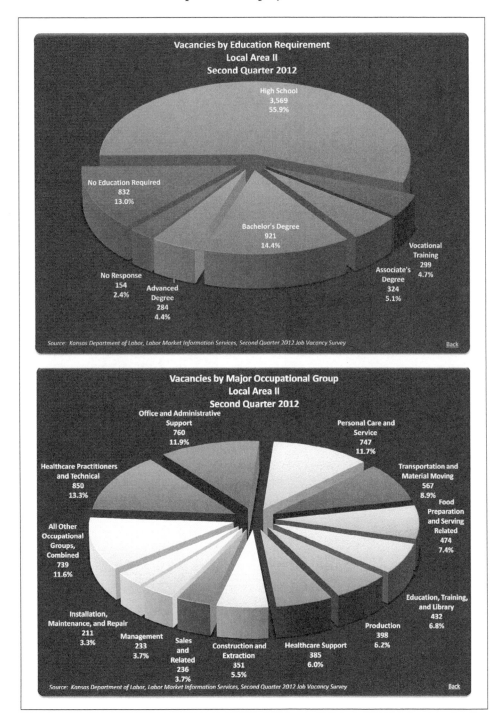

Vacancies by Education Requirement
Local Area II
Second Quarter 2012

High School
3,569
55.9%

No Education Required
832
13.0%

Bachelor's Degree
921
14.4%

Vocational Training
299
4.7%

Associate's Degree
324
5.1%

No Response
154
2.4%

Advanced Degree
284
4.4%

Source: Kansas Department of Labor, Labor Market Information Services, Second Quarter 2012 Job Vacancy Survey   Back

Vacancies by Major Occupational Group
Local Area II
Second Quarter 2012

Office and Administrative Support
760
11.9%

Personal Care and Service
747
11.7%

Healthcare Practitioners and Technical
850
13.3%

Transportation and Material Moving
567
8.9%

Food Preparation and Serving Related
474
7.4%

All Other Occupational Groups, Combined
739
11.6%

Education, Training, and Library
432
6.8%

Installation, Maintenance, and Repair
211
3.3%

Management
233
3.7%

Sales and Related
236
3.7%

Construction and Extraction
351
5.5%

Healthcare Support
385
6.0%

Production
398
6.2%

Source: Kansas Department of Labor, Labor Market Information Services, Second Quarter 2012 Job Vacancy Survey   Back

Figure 5.3
Sample State Employment Data *(cont'd)*

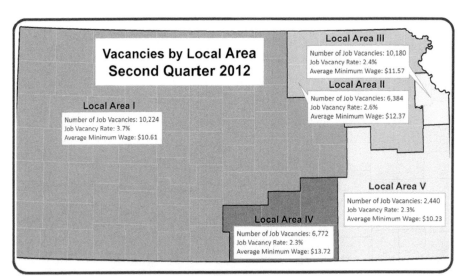

Source: Kansas Department of Labor, Labor Market Information Services, Second Quarter 2012 Job Vacancy Survey   Back

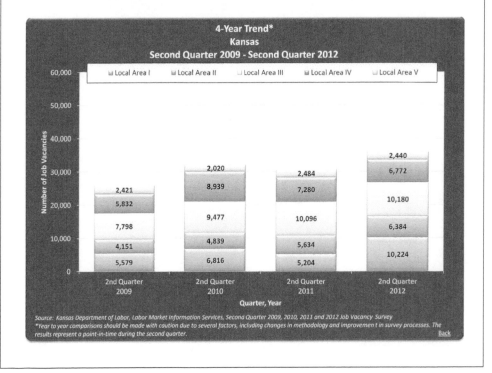

Source: Kansas Department of Labor, Labor Market Information Services, Second Quarter 2009, 2010, 2011 and 2012 Job Vacancy Survey
*Year to year comparisons should be made with caution due to several factors, including changes in methodology and improvement in survey processes. The results represent a point-in-time during the second quarter.   Back

23

Strategy 23: Gather Information and Collect Data

In other examples we have examined, such as postschool outcomes data, the data have identified a need for intervention. However, sometimes an already-observable need drives teams to collect more data. The necessary data and the strategies used for collection often depend on the nature of the need. Using the teaming strategies already in place, you can come up with various plans to acquire the data necessary to begin solving a problem. Below are three examples of how transition teams have developed surveys and organized research teams to acquire data to address challenges they have faced in their communities.

For example, during their involvement in a training program, one community transition team in a small, rural school district recognized that they had very few partnerships with local businesses to offer employment opportunities to their students. In their area, the only businesses offering traditional after-school jobs for high school students were a large chain grocery store and a restaurant. How could these two businesses possibly offer enough opportunities to support all of their students? To address this need, they realized they needed more data. Not only did they need to find more businesses or organizations that would offer employment experiences for their students, but they needed to form relationships with those businesses that would be willing to work with students with disabilities in their district.

Rather than beginning with informal networking, their first step was to brainstorm possible employers that could offer employment experiences to their high school students. Obviously, the team hadn't been able to identify a variety of possibilities on their own, so they enlisted the help of their students. High school students with disabilities that would directly benefit from more employment experiences worked with community transition team members to scour the phone books for possible partner organizations. Team members found that students were much more creative in the possibilities they saw for employment experiences. The list of possible organizations created by students included not only traditional sources of employment, like the nearby chain store and restaurant, but also unlikely candidates, such as local farmers, community organizations and churches, even elderly citizens who might need help with yard work or chores. When they completed their list, students had come up with almost 200 local entities that might be willing to offer employment experience to students with disabilities in their district.

Now that they had a more impressive pool of possible employers from which to choose, the community transition team needed to know what kind of experiences these entities might be willing to offer their students. Together, they developed a survey with a variety of possible activities on which individuals, organizations, and businesses could collaborate with schools. These included field trips, job shadowing, paid or unpaid summer internships, and paid part-time work during the school year. With the help of students enrolled in special education classes, surveys were mailed to the list of 200 identified possible employers. The team was surprised to find that almost 50 local entities were willing to participate in some way. The overwhelmingly positive response led the team to share the data with others in their district, thus also facilitating job experiences for students in the general education population.

After hearing from several of her former students, one educator we know who provides transition services noticed that those students attending the local community college were having difficulty passing some of their classes in their first year. Deciding to look into it further, she developed a survey to send to graduates with disabilities at both community colleges and four-year universities to gain more insight into the areas they struggled with during their first year. The survey contained questions such as "In which academic areas do you feel you have had the most difficulty in your first year of college or university?" and "On a 1-5 scale, with one being not at all and five being very effectively prepared, how prepared did you feel to balance your study time with your other responsibilities?" In the survey, the educator who provides transition services also provided a list of skills. This list included items such as note-taking, time management, study strategies, and research and organization skills. She asked respondents to check the ones they felt would have helped them to be more successful in their first year of school. She noticed that many students indicated that they struggled in preparing for tests, and the same students indicated that stronger note-taking and study strategies would have been helpful to them. In response to this analysis, the coordinator began implementing increased transition assessment in study skills and self-monitoring, and began developing additional curricula and collecting resources for test preparation. Next, she incorporated a transition activity for several students that involved visiting the local community college and meeting with the disability services coordinator. There, the students learned about the variety of services available on campus, from accommodations that would be available to them to the variety of tutoring programs and study groups the college had available. Following her efforts, she kept a close eye on postschool outcomes data to see if former students were more successful completing their first year.

Another community transition team in a small college town in the Midwest recognized a need for more housing options for transition-age students in their community. In an effort to increase the independent living outcomes of their students, the team mobilized to begin collecting data. Collectively, the team made an inventory of available housing that would be open to young people with disabilities, which included:

- Approximately 21 landlords in the community that accepted Section 8 vouchers.
- One apartment complex that offered one-bedroom apartments for seniors and individuals with disabilities.
- Another apartment complex that offered one-bedroom apartments for people over the age of 55.
- A total of 80 vouchers for nonelderly persons and families with disabilities (NED).

Their review of available housing confirmed that there were very few options for transition-age youth with disabilities. The long waiting period for Section 8 vouchers and the low number of NED vouchers, as well as the requirement of rental history for many low-income housing options, made them less-than-ideal choices for youth who would soon graduate high school and wish to live independently. So, the team began to research other options, joining with a nonprofit that worked to expand affordable housing options in their community, the transition team helped research possible programs and grants that could be used toward increasing affordable housing. The community transition team found that they could assist the nonprofit in applying for several sources of funds, including the HOME Investment Partnerships Program, Federal Home Loan Bank grants, as well as tax credits. The non-profit, with the team's support, was able to use these funds to develop rental properties for individuals and households with low incomes and disabilities, with several of the properties being universally accessible.

At this point, you may be thinking to yourself, "That last example sounds a lot like community resource mapping." If so, you are correct: community resource mapping is a method of data collection. See, you may have already been conducting independent data collection without even knowing it.

Roadblock Alert 3

Often we can be frustrated by low response rates to our surveys. There are a variety of strategies you can use to increase the number of people participating in your survey. This will give you more robust, reliable data on your community. Here are some strategies that your team can use to increase participation in survey collection:

- If possible, send students to collect responses in person
- Get students involved in writing personal letters to potential respondents
- Get parents involved in data collection; parents can have community connections that go beyond those other transition team members might have
- Collect data at school events such as at plays or athletic events
- Post links to surveys on your school or district website
- Distribute surveys along with district newsletters
- Utilize relationships you might have with former students to reach out to graduates

Figure 5.4
Sample Community Transition Team Survey

Please answer the following questions concerning your school's transition program.

1. I am familiar with the SAMPLE Community Transition Team and its activities.
   Strongly Agree ◯ Agree ◯ No ◯ Opinion ◯ Disagree ◯ Strongly Disagree ◯

2. I am confident that my school's transition program meets the State Standards and Indicators.
   Strongly Agree ◯ Agree ◯ No ◯ Opinion ◯ Disagree ◯ Strongly Disagree ◯

3. I am confident that my school's transition program meets the needs of our students.
   Strongly Agree ◯ Agree ◯ No ◯ Opinion ◯ Disagree ◯ Strongly Disagree ◯

4. I would be interested in having another teacher from the Community Transition Team act as a mentor or contact person.
   Strongly Agree ◯ Agree ◯ No ◯ Opinion ◯ Disagree ◯ Strongly Disagree ◯

5. I would like to have more information about the following transition topics (choose all that apply):

   a. Transition Assessments ◯
   b. Transition Curriculum/Job Skills Training ◯
   c. Missouri Connections ◯
   d. Transition Standards and Indicators ◯
   e. Student-directed IEPs ◯
   f. Student work experiences ◯
   g. Indicator 13 ◯
   h. Other (please specify) ◯

6. The Community Transition Team has sponsored a Transition Fair the past 2 years. What could be done differently to encourage greater participation by schools, students, and parents?

7. What other services do you think the Community Transition Team could provide?

8. Which agencies do you routinely include in your transition IEP meetings (as needed)? (Choose all that apply.)

   a. Vocational Rehabilitation ◯
   b. Mental Health services ◯
   c. PTI (Parent Training Information Center) ◯
   d. Armed Services ◯
   e. College Representative ◯
   f. Vo-Tech Representative ◯
   g. Employer ◯
   h. Community Services ◯
   i. Other (please specify) ◯

9. Please make any other comments. If you are interested in working more closely with the Sample Community Transition Team, please contact (e-mail and name).

Activity 23.1: Create Your Own Survey

There are several strategies that can be used to create surveys for yourself (see Figure 5.4) or adapt surveys from other sources. One very powerful strategy can be the utilization of online survey services. SurveyMonkey (http://www.surveymonkey.com) is a popular online survey service. Their basic package allows for short, 10-question surveys with 15 different question types, and will allow you to collect a total of 100 responses per survey. It also offers more advanced paid packages, which might be useful if you are planning to design and disseminate longer surveys to large audiences. Google Forms, part of Google Drive (formerly Google Docs), can also be useful for distributing surveys. A guide to creating Google Forms is currently available at the following web address: http://support. google.com/drive/bin/answer.py?hl=en&answer=87809. For the less technologically inclined, distributing a paper survey can be the most effective way to collect data.

Conclusion

Data is the key to getting an accurate picture of your unique situation. It can shed light on postschool outcomes, academic achievement, employment opportunities, or any number of other factors your team is interested in. With more information, your team will be able to focus its efforts and provide the most relevant transition assistance possible.

Chapter 6

Sustaining Collaborative Efforts

Have you ever been a part of a team or collaborative effort that started out strong, but ended after only a few months or a year of effort? Sustained change can be difficult to achieve. Many a team starts out with the intention of longevity and the support of energetic members, but the effort dwindles and falls apart over time. *Sustainability* can be defined as continuing improvement practices over time through needs assessment, action planning, and ongoing improvement.

Because sustaining change can be difficult, it's important to plan to be around for a long time—right from the beginning. Certain attributes have been identified that contribute to long-term collaborative teams, including:

- Participants view team activities as effective and meaningful.
- Leadership effectively promotes and supports collaboration.
- Team receives political support at local and state levels.
- Members benefit from continual, high-quality professional development or assistance.
- Processes for ongoing evaluation or monitoring of success are in place.
- Team receives community support (Florian, 2000, p. 12).

This chapter presents strategies specific to sustaining your collaboration and teaming effort:

- Strategy 24:   Plan For Sustainability
- Strategy 25:   Develop Bylaws
- Strategy 26:   Develop a Memorandum of Understanding

It is important to note that strategies throughout this book should not be viewed in isolation, and that these are not the only strategies that promote sustainability. Strategies presented in prior chapters contribute to individual collaboration as well as building and maintaining a high-functioning, activity-oriented team. If your team has not developed high levels of collaboration and functioning, sustainability will be difficult to achieve.

24

Strategy 24: Plan for Sustainability

In order to ensure sustainability, start planning for your team's future early. Of course, you can't create your sustainability plan at your first meeting, because you won't have a good idea of your team's unique strengths or the challenges you will face. You may, however, want to incorporate an annual sustainability assessment into your team's agenda. For example, you may decide that the end of the school year marks an ideal point to plan for sustainability, and could schedule the assessment to recur every year at that time. Annual reassessments are important, because your strengths, challenges, and mission may change slightly over time. There are several activities your team can undertake to help create a sustainability plan.

Activity 24.1: Identify Sustainability Strengths and Barriers

One strategy to develop and maintain a functioning team is to have members reflect on sustainability strengths and areas of concern. Pose specific questions to the team at a meeting: What capacities, resources, policies, or practices contribute to the team's success? What has hindered or presented a challenge to its work? Write down everyone's answer (you can use large sheets of paper or a whiteboard) so that all answers are shared and discussed, and summarize the responses.

1. *Sustainability Strengths:* When you think about your community transition team accomplishments, what *capacities, resources, policies or practices* contributed to your success?
2. *Sustainability Barriers:* Has anything hindered your teamwork?

Table 6.1 presents the results of this activity for three real community transition teams. As you can see, each team came up with different strengths and barriers based on their specific assets and challenges.

Once you have identified your strengths and challenges, your team will be better equipped to complete the sustainability survey and create sustainability goals. These activities will enable your team to reflect on its current practices and create concrete plans to help ensure sustainability.

Activity 24.2: Administer the Sustainability Survey

Have each team member individually complete the Sustainability Survey and Sustained Teaming Activities Checklist (see Figure 6.1, Appendix, Tool #9). Once all members have completed the scale, aggregating the results will give you an idea of your team's overall level of confidence in its future. Discuss each question as a group, paying close attention to low-scoring items.

Table 6.1
Sustainability Strengths and Barriers

TEAM	SUSTAINABILITY STRENGTHS	SUSTAINABILITY BARRIERS
Alpha Transition Team	Vision Commitment Family/parent involvement	Overcommitment Not communicating clearly No follow-through Stepping on toes Lack of time
Southwest Community Transition Team	Determination Membership Enthusiasm Knowledge Awareness Employer commitment and agencies Changing quality of life Variety of resources	Change of leadership Not listening Not following through No consistency One or two not doing their share Personalities (narrow minded, opinionated people) Too fast Don't measure what matters
Northern Lights Community Transition Team	Membership Commitment Communication Networking Value Enthusiasm Buy-in	Losing key players/team members Lack of follow-through Inability to bring new partners on Demands and pressures of current jobs/too busy Agency assumptions

Once you have figured out areas to work on for sustainability, refer to Tool #9's list of activities that promote sustained teaming. Use your identified weaknesses to select the items that you think your team should consider as an activity for a sustainability action plan. Once you have selected three to five items, discuss the possibility of including each one in your action plan.

Figure 6.1
Sample Sustainability Survey Feedback

ITEM	RATING
How confident are you that your team will achieve your team goals?	1 2 3 ④ 5
Why? We have great enthusiasm, but I worry about turnover of members.	
How confident are you that your team will share responsibility in implementing activities?	1 2 3 4 ⑤
Why or why not? We always work together + share the workload!	
How confident are you that the transition team will produce lasting benefits for each team member's agency?	1 2 ③ 4 5
Why? I think we will have great results for most agencies – not sure about VR.	
How confident are you that your CTT will be around for 6 months?	1 2 3 4 ⑤
Why? We should be set for the rest of the year.	
How confident are you that your CTT will be around for 1 year?	1 2 ③ 4 5
Why? Key members are leaving at the end of this year.	
How confident are you that your CTT will be around for 5 years?	1 ② 3 4 5
Why? If we can get through this round of people leaving, we should be OK.	

Activity 24.3: Develop Sustainability Goals

As a group, it's important to include goals for sustainability as part of your working action plan (see Chapter 4). Using your results from the Sustainability Survey, determine which activities you would like to include as goals and develop action steps for each goal. What steps need to take place within the next 1 to 6 months in order to reach each sustainability goal? Who needs to be involved in completing each goal? You may wish to consult Strategy 18 for more guidance on how to create an action plan. Your team's sustainability goals may or may not overlap with your existing action plan goals, but they must always focus on strengthening your team in some way.

Table 6.2 presents the sustainability goals and action plan items created by a real community transition team. The action plan items outline the specific steps the transition team planned to take to accomplish their sustainability goal.

The following examples detail various goals and solutions created by real community transition teams. These goals range from increased funding to increased outreach, but all goals connect to teams' sustainability efforts.

EXAMPLE: Apply for Funding

In one example of a community transition team creating sustainability goals, a KansasOne community transition team formed a short-term task force to identify the support needs for youth with disabilities who remained in school through the age of 21. After using Activity 22.1 to conduct an analysis of postschool outcomes, they determined that the current instructional design was not working. These youth were being taught in self-contained classes within the high school and received no community-based instruction. The community transition team determined that external funding was necessary to significantly improve the instructional design. Through collaboration with a local university, they applied for a federal grant to develop a mentoring project; they also applied for a state grant to develop a work-based internship in their community and for a collaborative grant through the local technical school to provide independent living courses. Finally, they also applied for a local community development grant to support interagency coordination of services. The community received all four grants, and within 2 years there was an array of options for these young adults, all designed to meet each student's unique needs. The community transition team attributed its success to the comprehensive needs assessment and the representation of different stakeholders within the team.

In addition to seeking funding for transition team projects through grants, consider turning to the community for help. One team created a flyer (see Figure 6.2) to gain funding for a community employment initiative. Notice that the flyer includes professional-looking graphics and logos; when asking for financial support, be sure your program comes across as legitimate, organized, and worthy of support.

Table 6.2
Sample Sustainability Goals and Action Plan Items

SUSTAINABILITY GOAL	ACTION PLAN ITEMS
Develop: mission, vision, case for support	❏ Tallk with community partners and stakeholders about outcomes of year 1. ❏ Review progress toward goals, who will benefit, and who else needs to be involved. ❏ Review community needs and trends. ❏ Revise mission and vision as necessary.
Research and identify potential sources of funding	❏ Research local businesses, foundations, and other givers who have an interest in our cause. ❏ Solicit ideas from partners, staff, volunteers, and the advisory committee about contacts they might have to potential givers who share interests with our CTT.
Use public relations to improve visibility and secure community support	❏ Talk to local businesses and each other about how the CTT can benefit their interests. Ask for their ideas. ❏ Identify any products/ services of our CTT that are valued in the community and could produce assistance or help to offset expenses or other issues. ❏ Create a team plan, and even a marketing plan if needed. ❏ Cultivate relationships, even with media if it would be helpful. ❏ Identify possible partners we need to communicate with, or how our communications could cover a broader group (the web?).

Figure 6.2
Sample Fundraising Flyer

EXAMPLE: CTT Brochure

Another community transition team determined that they were not communicating effectively with the community. The team had a lot of exciting initiatives up and running, but participation was not as good as they had hoped, and community members didn't seem to know about any of their efforts. In order to raise awareness, they created promotional material (see Figure 6.3) describing their initiatives. Through this public relations effort, they were able to not only improve participation in their programs but also gain support to help sustain these and other activities in the future.

Figure 6.3
Sample Organization Brochure

EXAMPLE: Press Release

One way to maintain a profile in the community is to send out regular press releases (see Chapter 2) about programs and initiatives (see Figure 6.4 for sample). Press releases should focus on *team* accomplishments, rather than individual or school-based subjects. When your team accomplishes exciting things, be sure to let the community know. Press releases encourage your members to take pride in their achievements while simultaneously spreading the word about new opportunities for students with disabilities. Increasing the transition team's community presence is a very common sustainability goal, so don't hold back when it comes to publicizing your successes.

Figure 6.4
Sample Press Release

FOR IMMEDIATE RELEASE
SWAT Program a "Model of Success"

West Plains—December 10, 2011—Westview School District's Students Working at Transition (SWAT) Program at Williams College, which began in September, has been cited as a "Model of Success" by the state Department of Education.

All students in the program receive special education services and are 16 years of age or older. Students work at the college when school is not in session, generally for about half of a regular work day.

"Setting high expectations early in life helps students develop the skills to succeed in the future," said Marie Gonzalez, who supervises several students in the college's registrar's office. One of the student's counselor's noted that "Work-based learning is one way students can identify interests, strengths, skills, and needs related to career development."

Real-world work experiences provide youth with an opportunity to develop not only work skills but also an understanding of the workplace. Students in the program are expected to meet typical work standards, including arriving on time, being a team player, showing respect for self and others, staying on task, dressing appropriately, and being reliable.

The SWAT program is seeking additional business and community partners, to expand opportunities for students in the program.

Contact:
Joe Davis
jdavis21@sample.net

No matter what your team's sustainability goals are, it is important to review them periodically and make sure they are still relevant. As you address some sustainability needs, be aware that circumstances may change to create new challenges. Sustainability planning is an ongoing activity that needs to be repeated frequently in order to keep your team at peak performance.

25

Strategy 25: Develop Bylaws

Establishing bylaws can be a key mechanism to ensure your community transition team continues. Bylaws are an official document describing the governance of your organization. Bylaws provide clear and specific guidance about how your team operates; these rules can prove invaluable when faced with retirement and turnover of administrators, teachers, and adult service agency staff. When developing bylaws, include any information that would be critical if leadership were to leave suddenly. Bylaws are similar to ground rules in that they describe how your community transition team functions and what it means to be a member. The key to sustaining a community transition team is to plan for sustainability, maintain membership, remain action-oriented, and function well as a team.

Activity 25.1: Create Bylaws

Developing bylaws doesn't have to be time-consuming, and it doesn't require attention from the entire team. To create bylaws, form a committee of five or fewer people, most of whom have years of experience with the organization but including one to two novice members to ensure a new team member perspective. The bylaws committee is a short-term, working committee, existing for the sole purpose of developing the bylaws document. After initial development, the draft should be presented to all team members for discussion, refinement to add clarity, and voting for approval. After the bylaws are adopted, each team member should be given a copy. When new team members join, they should be given a copy of the bylaws as part of their introduction to the team. In addition, plan to review the bylaws periodically; you may want to add or delete committees.

The primary purpose of bylaws is to maintain a single document that includes the mission statement, describes officers' roles and responsibilities, and specifies how the team will reach consensus during decision-making. Bylaws should include information such as:

- *Name and purpose* (vision statement) of your community transition team. How will the team promote positive postschool outcomes for youth? As appropriate, also include information about community strengths and needs.
- *Titles and duties* of each officer (e.g., Chair, Co-Chair, Treasurer, Communications Officer). Identify the process of how officers are chosen and terms of service.
- *Schedule for meetings*, meeting times and places, and attendance rules.
- *Name of each committee* with clear purpose of committee.

To summarize, the primary purpose of bylaws is to maintain a single document for the vision/mission statement, to describe officers' roles and responsibilities, and to specify how the team will reach consensus during decision-making. If your team decides against formal bylaws, it would be helpful to at least create a document describing how you are organized. Putting this information in writing formalizes and provides structure to your

team and helps establish equity among the members. Tool #10 in the Appendix is a
sample of bylaws similar to those used by other community transition teams.

Strategy 26: Develop a Memorandum of Understanding

A memorandum of understanding (MOU) can be thought of as a formal interagency
agreement that clearly outlines the relationship between agencies, and can be a key
strategy for interagency collaboration. MOUs provide mechanisms for communication
and referral of students, and can promote activities such as shared funding and joint
training. In addition, they formalize relationships between various agencies such as a
local education agency, vocational rehabilitation (VR) provider, and disability organization. They occur at both the local and state levels.

26

At the state level, MOUs are sometimes developed to provide guidelines for sharing
local-level resources. For example, in one state, an MOU was developed between two
agencies to form a new service provision to provide at-risk students and students with
mild disabilities with vocational training and assessment through community colleges
across the state. In another state, an educator who provides transition services noted that:

> We have very clearly set the expectation [for interagency collaboration]
> through our memorandum of understanding…. These relationships
> are improving dramatically [and] there's an expectation of cooperation
> from the highest level right on through the system. There are a lot of
> opportunities [for collaboration] out there because of the expectation.

The development process serves as a key activity for relationship building, because
it requires that participants share information and work on common goals. In one state,
the MOU team went on to provide joint regional trainings and developed resources to
improve collaboration at the local level. In another state, three agencies who had recently
updated the state-level MOU reported that they would be "taking that on the road this
fall to talk about the state agreement between the three agencies and what that means for
successful transition for students regarding work, employment, and Title I eligibility, as
well as general provisions for VR."

At the local level, there are a lot of different interagency agreements. Whereas some
only involve two parties, such as Vocational Rehabilitation and the school district, others
are much more comprehensive and involve multiple entities such as SSA, Labor, postsecondary education, the district, VR, the Department of Health, and so forth. MOUs are
developed at the administrative level, and they frequently delineate agency responsibilities. One educator who provides transition services described the MOU as

> a mutual agreement to provide services under certain stipulated
> conditions…. Each high school has quite a bit of freedom within that
> MOU to outline the specifics in terms of deadlines, steps to be taken
> that work for that high school…. I appreciate that flexibility to arrive
> at custom-tailored arrangements for delivery of services.

An administrator in another district explained how the transition team developed "an agreement signed by middle-level management and the directors" that was updated every 2 years and included agencies and organizations in the fields of mental health, services for the blind, and supporting individuals with intellectual and developmental disabilities. The MOU identified points of contact for each agency, outlined potential services and eligibility requirements, and provided a formal commitment to working together.

Activity 26.1: Develop an MOU

When developing relationships with agencies critical to your purpose, discuss how a formalized relationship would be beneficial to implementation of services. Work together to draft the MOU; you should include:

- *Representative names and entities*: List all agencies participating in the interagency agreement. (e.g., Vocational Rehabilitation Services, Department of Labor and Workforce Development, Division of Developmental Disabilities)
- Describe the reason for the MOU (e.g., increased number of transition-age youth transitioning to employment, state statistics) and definitions of population served.
- *Scope:* Describe the roles and responsibilities of each entity (e.g., designate a contact person, establish referral process) and things all entities will do (e.g., work well together, communicate).
- *Eligibility:* Include eligibility information for each entity's target population (optional).
- *Signatures:* Have administrators from each entity sign and date the MOU. Include complete contact information (e-mails and phone numbers).

MOUs are a common way to formalize interagency relationships at both the state and local levels; they are used to identify responsibilities and services of multiple agencies and provide a framework for collaboration. MOUs also serve as a vehicle for relationship building, from the time of initial development of the MOU. Figure 6.5 is an example of an MOU that outlines the relationship between a school district and an local employer.

Conclusion

Implementing sustainability strategies will help your team continue its work for many, many years. Don't forget that in this rapidly changing world, the context in which your team operates is also always changing. Our goal in this book has been to make this information easily accessible so you can return to it as a reference at any time. To that end, the next section, the appendix, contains blank versions of all the tools presented throughout this book.

Figure 6.5
Sample Memorandum of Understanding

Community Based Vocational Instruction (CBVI)
Master Agreement

This Master Agreement made between ███████████████████████ a Missouri public body, herein after called ████████████████ and ---, a Missouri corporation/business, hereinafter called "---", shall be effective July 1, 2011.

WITNESSETH THAT:

WHEREAS, the parties hereto desire to cooperate in establishing a site for a Community Based Vocational/Instruction, whereby ██████████████ may utilize specified vocational experiences offered by ---.

WHEREAS, --- is willing to make available volunteer work experiences to ██████████████

NOW, THEREFORE, in consideration of mutual promises hereinafter contained, the parties hereby agree as follows:

I. ████████████████████████████ **TO:**

    A. Adhere to the defined components of the program as set forth in the Community Based Vocational/Instruction Program (CBVI Program), as approved for the school year.

    B. Assume responsibility for the overall administration of the CBVI Program;
        1. evaluation, selection and coordination of students for the CBVI Program, and
        2. provision of faculty for on-going coordination with ---.

    C. Withdraw from the CBVI Program any student or faculty member when it is determined by ██████████████ that the student or faculty member is undesirable for reasons of health, performance, or other reasonable cause.

    D. Maintain policies providing that the students and faculty abide by the rules and regulations of --- while performing activities pursuant to this Master Agreement, and providing that students and faculty will not enter locations or engage in any activities not authorized by --- staff.

    E. Assume the responsibility for any injury, destruction, or damage to any person or property caused by student or faculty while participating in the program as a result of their direct negligence, in relation to --- while on --- premises. However, such responsibility is limited to the amount of any insurance coverage maintained by the ██████████████ for the act of omission in question.

    F. Provide comprehensive general liability insurance for faculty during the term of the Master Agreement for a minimum of $1,000,000 per occurrence and $2,000,000 per year in the aggregate. Such insurance will not be canceled or materially altered unless --- is notified in writing thirty (30) days prior to such action. Any decrease in the limits outlined above, unless approved by --- would require termination of the Master Agreement.

Revised 8/11   1

Figure 6.5
Sample Memorandum of Understanding *(cont'd)*

G. ▆▆▆▆▆▆▆▆▆ shall maintain workers' compensation insurance covering any liability it might incur under the Missouri Workers' Compensation Law which arises out of injuries sustained by its employees and including employer's liability insurance.

H. Notwithstanding anything contained herein to the contrary, the▆▆▆▆▆▆▆ does not herein waive any right of sovereign immunity available to the▆▆▆▆▆ ▆▆▆▆ under the laws of the State of Missouri.

II. --- AGREES TO:

A. Provide work training in designated areas for students. The number of students, hours, and days of the week for training are to be mutually agreed upon by▆▆▆▆▆▆. ▆▆▆▆ and ---.

B. Provide basic job descriptions and orientations to the designated work training positions with follow-up supervision to assure that job duties are efficiently and effectively carried out.

C. Assume responsibility for explaining to and instructing its staff in their respective roles and relationships with the students and faculty of▆▆▆▆▆▆▆▆▆▆

D. Provide an orientation to the rules and regulations of --- for the faculty of▆▆▆▆▆▆ ▆▆▆▆

E. As needed and based upon the availability of ---, provide accommodating classroom space for students and faculty.

III. IT IS MUTUALLY AGREED BY BOTH PARTIES THAT:

A. --- has the right to request removal from the CBVI Program outlined in this Master Agreement any student or faculty that it feels has not complied with the rules and regulations of ---, (including all personnel rules and policies applicable to staff).

B. Neither party shall, in the operation of the Master Agreement, unlawfully discriminate against any individual on the basis of race, religion, sex, creed, national origin or physical or intellectual disability.

C. Under no circumstances is the student or faculty of▆▆▆▆▆▆▆▆▆▆ to be considered an agent or employee of --- while engaged in the CBVI Program activities as defined in this Master Agreement.

Revised 8/11   2

Figure 6.5
Sample Memorandum of Understanding *(cont'd)*

D. The parties agree they will share responsibility for ensuring their CBVI Program fully complies with the U. S. Department of Labor and U. S. Department of Education Guidelines for Implementation of Community-Based Education Programs for Students with Disabilities. To ensure full compliance with these Guidelines, the parties agree that each party will have the following responsibilities:

████████████████ shall be responsible for ensuring compliance with the following Guidelines:

1. Participants will be youth with physical and/or intellectual disabilities for whom competitive employment at or above the minimum wage level is not immediately obtainable and who, because of their disability, will need intensive on-going support to perform in a work setting.
2. Participation will be for vocational exploration, assessment or training in a community-based placement worksite under the general supervision of public school personnel.
3. Community-based placements will be clearly defined components of individual education programs developed and designed for the benefit of each student. The statement of needed transition services established for exploration, assessment or training or cooperative vocational education components will be included in the students' Individualized Education Program (IEP).
4. Information contained in a student's IEP will not automatically have to be made available to the Department of Labor, however, documentation that reflects the student and his or her parent or guardian is fully informed of the IEP and the community-based placement component, have indicated voluntary participation, and understand that participation in such component does not entitle the student-participant to wages will be provided to the Department of Labor upon request.
5. Such placements are made according to the requirements of the student's IEP and not to meet the labor needs of the business.
6. The periods of time spent by the students at any one site or in any clearly distinguishable job classification are specifically limited by the IEP.

If the U.S. Department of Labor, U.S. Department of Education, or any other person or entity initiates an investigation or brings a claim, proceeding, or lawsuit against --- based on an alleged action or omission under the Fair Labor Standards Act based on failure to comply with one of the six requirements immediately above, for which ████████████████ is responsible for ensuring compliance, then ████████████████ shall defend and fully indemnify --- in that investigation, proceeding, or lawsuit.

--- shall be responsible for ensuring compliance with the following guidelines:

Revised 8/11

3

Figure 6.5
Sample Memorandum of Understanding *(cont'd)*

1. The activities of the student at the community-based placement site do not result in an immediate advantage to the business.
2. There has been no displacement of employees, vacant positions have not been filled with students rather than employees, employees have not been relieved of assigned duties, and the students are not performing services that, although not ordinarily performed by employees, clearly are of benefit to the business.
3. The students are not under continued and direct supervision of employees of ⸻ rather than of representatives of the school.
4. Students are not entitled to employment at ⸻ at the conclusion of their IEP. However, if a student becomes an employee of ⸻, the student cannot be considered a trainee at ⸻ unless in a different, clearly distinguishable occupation.
5. Each component will not exceed the following limitation during any one school year:

   - Vocational exploration   5 hours per job experience
   - Vocational assessment   90 hours per job experience
   - Vocational training   120 hours per job experience

IV. TERM AND TERMINATION

The term of this Master Agreement shall be for one (1) year from the effective date of the Master Agreement, however, this Master Agreement shall be automatically renewed for one (1) year periods unless canceled by thirty (30) days written notice by either party in advance of annual termination date.

V. ADDENDUM TO THIS MASTER AGREEMENT

Where applicable and if mutually agreed upon by both parties, an addendum to the Master Agreement may be made to evidence associated branches/stores/locations. When needed, such addendum will be attached as an appendix, in the form of attached Appendix A, and can be added with other signatures. The addendum is subject to all of the conditions described therein. The purpose is to incorporate into the Master Agreement, branches/stores/locations associated with the original party where students will be participating in training activities.

Appendix

Tool #1:   Transition Collaboration Strategies Strengths and Weaknesses
Tool #2:   Teaching Practices Supporting College and Career Readiness
Tool #3:   Transition Assessment Framework
Tool #4:   Meeting Agenda
Tool #5:   Process Checklist
Tool #6:   Team Functioning Scale
Tool #7:   Action Plan Template
Tool #8:   Shared Leadership Survey
Tool #9:   Sustainability Survey and Sustained Teaming Activities Checklist
Tool #10: Sample Bylaws

Tool #1: Transition Collaboration Strategies Strengths and Weaknesses

Purpose: This checklist allows transition professionals to quickly reflect on their strengths and areas of need as they work toward collaborating with their colleagues and other members of their community.

Instructions: Review each item, writing a plus sign by your areas of strength and a minus sign by areas of need. If numerous areas of need exist, it may be helpful to prioritize the needs.

+ OR -	TRANSITION COLLABORATION STRATEGIES
	1. I have a clear understanding of how my co-workers' jobs are related to transition.
	2. I have a clear understanding of a variety of adult agency services that young adults with disabilities may access.
	3. I feel that my boss supports transition education/services.
	4. I communicate information about transition to co-workers within my school/organization.
	5. I communicate information about transition to colleagues from outside my school/organization.
	6. I communicate frequently with families about transition planning and services.
	7. On a regular basis, I coordinate transition services with co-workers in my school/organization.
	8. I regularly work with staff outside my school/organization to coordinate transition services.
	9. I participate in professional development related to transition.
	10. I participate in professional development outside my organization where I learn ways to improve transition practices.

Note. Adapted with permission from Transition Collaboration Survey, by P. Noonan, A. Gaumer Erickson, and M. Morningstar. Copyright 2012 by the Center for Research on Learning, University of Kansas.

Tool #2: Teaching Practices Supporting College and Career Readiness

Purpose: This survey identifies elements of college and career readiness that are in place within a school. It supports school teams as they plan for continued and improved implementation of college and career readiness.

Instructions: Have each person completing the survey answer the demographic data and then rate each indicator or leave the response blank if the item is not applicable to their role in the school. For access to the complete survey, please contact Dr. Amy Gaumer Erickson, aerickson@ku.edu.

Role: ☐ General Education Teacher

☐ Special Education Teacher

☐ Administrator

☐ Counselor

☐ Other (please identify): _____

Subject(s) Taught: _____

District/School: _____

Years at the School: ☐ 0-1

☐ 2-5

☐ 6-10

☐ More than 10

Tool #2: Teaching Practices Supporting College and Career Readiness (cont'd)

Student Engagement in College & Career Readiness For this section, think about all of the students that you interact with or instruct.	
(5) All Students (4) Most Students (3) Some Students (2) Few Students (1) No Students	
1. Students enter 9th grade with an awareness of their learning styles.	5 4 3 2 1
2. Students enter 9th grade with an awareness of their career interests and skills.	5 4 3 2 1
7. At least annually, students complete career interest/knowledge assessments and review the results.	5 4 3 2 1
8. Students explore career requirements for careers of interest (e.g., prerequisites, required training, availability).	5 4 3 2 1
9. Students have opportunities to practice employment-related skills within the school (e.g., school business, resume development, mock interviews, conflict resolution).	5 4 3 2 1

Teaching Practices Supporting College & Career Readiness For this section, think specifically about the course(s) that you teach. If you do not teach any courses, skip this section.	
(5) Regularly (4) (3) Occasionally (2) (1) Never	
16. I teach and support students to utilize study & test-taking skills within my course(s).	5 4 3 2 1
17. I teach my students strategies for effective decision making.	5 4 3 2 1
26. I monitor the academic progress of my students through ongoing assessment.	5 4 3 2 1
27. I implement multiple types of assessments within my course(s) (e.g., performance-based assessment, short answer, essay, multiple choice).	5 4 3 2 1
30. I review data on students' knowledge and skills with other professionals in my school.	5 4 3 2 1

Tool #2: Teaching Practices Supporting College and Career Readiness (cont'd)

School Infrastructure & Shared Vision Supporting College & Career Readiness For this section, consider all supports that are available to students within your school.					
(5) Completely in place (4) (3) Somewhat in place (2) (1) Not in place					
38. Within the school, individualized career-related opportunities and assessments are provided to students that are unsure of their postsecondary goals.	5	4	3	2	1
39. Families are provided with resources/information from my school to support college and career planning.	5	4	3	2	1
40. My curriculum is aligned to college- and career-readiness standards (e.g., Common Core, Core State Standards).	5	4	3	2	1
41. My curriculum is aligned vertically (across grade levels) to support students to progress to higher-level coursework.	5	4	3	2	1
42. My curriculum is aligned horizontally (across courses at the same grade level) to support students in transferring knowledge.	5	4	3	2	1
(5) Strongly Agree (4) Somewhat Agree (3) Neutral (2) Somewhat Disagree (1) Strongly Disagree					
51. My school has a positive school climate that is safe and respectful for all students.	5	4	3	2	1
52. My administrators are committed to implementing evidence-based instructional practices that support college- and career-readiness.	5	4	3	2	1
53. Students' families are engaged in academic decision-making and planning (e.g., course of study, individualized support).	5	4	3	2	1

Note. Reprinted with permission from Indicators of College and Career Readiness Survey, by A. Gaumer Erickson and P. Noonan. Copyright 2013 by the Center for Research on Learning, University of Kansas.

Tool #3: Transition Assessment Framework

Purpose: This framework assists school teams as they catalogue their transition assessments, identifying whether they are adequately implementing assessments in outcome areas.

Instructions: Use the Transition Assessment Framework to list the number and types of assessments you have for transition outcomes in employment, postsecondary education or training, and independent living.

CORE ASSESSMENTS			
	Assessment Title	Information Gained	When administered
Employment			
Education/ Training			
Independent Living			

Tool #3: Transition Assessment Framework (cont'd)

	SMALL GROUP/ELECTIVE ASSESSMENTS		
	Assessment Title	Information Gained	When administered
Employment			
Education/ Training			
Independent Living			

Tool #3: Transition Assessment Framework (cont'd)

	Assessment Title	Information Gained	When administered
INDIVIDUAL ASSESSMENTS			
Employment			
Education/ Training			
Independent Living			

Note. Reprinted with permission from Transition Assessment Framework by A. Gaumer Erickson. Copyright 2012 by the Center for Research on Learning, University of Kansas.

Tool #4: Meeting Agenda

Purpose: This template can be used as a guide for teams as they draft agendas and begin to plan the structure of their meetings.

Instructions: Use the following as a template for your meeting agendas, or as you develop your own agenda.

Facilitator		Date	
Location		Time	
Norms		Roles	
Attendees			

AGENDA ITEMS			
Who	Time	Items	Notes

Tool #4: Meeting Agenda (cont'd)

TO DO LIST			
No.	Item(s)	Person(s) responsible	Target Date
1.			
2.			
3.			
4.			
5.			
6.			
UPCOMING DATES			
Date:	Start/end times:	Team(s)/Conferences:	Location:

Note. Adapted with permission from Agenda Template for the Missouri SPDG Project Management Team by R. Jenson. Copyright 2012 by the Institute for Human Development, University of Missouri Kansas City.

Tool #5: Process Checklist

Purpose: This checklist can help teams to develop and sustain strong team structure as they reflect on whether common indicators of success are in place for their team.

Instructions: Teams should fill out the Process Checklist together at least once, but preferably two times per year, to ensure all 25 indicators are in place. If not, notes/action items are recorded by the team for immediate consideration and inclusion in an action plan.

COMMUNITY TRANSITION TEAM PROCESS CHECKLIST	I PLACE (YES/ NO)	NOTES/ACTION ITEMS
1.. Community transition team is established and includes critical representation based on community needs (e.g., school personnel, Centers for Independent Living, Department of Mental Health and Vocational Rehabilitation Counselor, family member, employer).		
2. Community transition team is representative of community and reflects community needs.		
3. Community transition team has established a team name and shared-vision with the expanded team through the Mini-Maps Process.		
4. Community transition team meets monthly at a minimum.		
5. Community transition team has identified community and transition areas of need and prioritized five major goals. Entire team is knowledgeable of these goals.		
6. Based on team goals, community transition team jointly developed an action plan that outlines activities based on their goals, as well as persons responsible and timeline that is reviewed at every meeting.		
7. Team norms or ground rules have been established and agreed upon.		
8. Meeting structure (i.e., agenda and timing) has been established and agreed upon.		
9. An organizational system for tracking meeting notes, materials, and data has been established and is maintained.		
10. A system of assigned or rotated roles is defined (e.g., facilitator, note-keeper, time-keeper) to assure high quality and effective meeting time.		

Tool #5: Process Checklist (cont'd)

11. Community transition team members have equal voice when planning team activities.		
12. Process for reaching a team decision (i.e. consensus or majority vote) has been defined and adopted.		
13. Building administration – that is, principal or district level administrator attends CTT team meeting at least 3x a year (e.g., Fall, Winter, Spring) and receives agenda and minutes for every meeting.		
14. Community transition team collaboratively reflects on areas of local need identified through data (e.g., Indicator 13 compliance data, dropout data, graduation rates, outcomes)		
15. Community transition team systematically uses data to drive decision-making.		
16. Community transition team systematically shares information with critical district-wide staff and administrators.		
17. Community transition team systematically shares transition information with community and families.		
18. Community transition team systematically communicates with surrounding districts on CTT initiatives.		
19. Transition-related professional development events are included on CTT meeting agendas for dissemination and discussion.		
20. At least annually, community transition team revisits and updates an action plan that addresses the prioritized needs identified through data analysis.		
21. District leadership is familiar with the contents of the action plan.		
22. CTT membership is reviewed at least annually and new members are recruited.		
23. A process is in place to welcome new members to team.		
24. Bylaws have been developed by CTT by Community Transition Team		
25. Sustainability plan has been developed by CTT and is revisited at least annually.		

Tool #6: Team Functioning Scale

Purpose: This scale can help teams to assess their current level of functioning, and identify areas on which they can improve.

Instructions: Complete the survey while considering your last three team meetings. Items on the left are examples of low team functioning, and corresponding items on the right represent high team functioning. Complete the sliding scale (1-5) between the items to relate your observed level of team functioning for your district team.

Structure	Meeting roles unassigned	1 2 3 4 5	Multiple meeting roles assigned prior to the meeting (e.g., facilitator, note-taker)
	Ever-changing start and stop times (e.g., members straggle in, waiting for leadership, meetings sometimes cancelled)	1 2 3 4 5	Meeting starts and ends on time as scheduled
	Irregular attendance by team members	1 2 3 4 5	Nearly all team members attend regularly
	Nonexistent or limited use of agendas	1 2 3 4 5	Agenda developed and available prior to meetings
	Nonexistent or limited use of meeting minutes/notes	1 2 3 4 5	Minutes/notes taken during meeting and distributed to all team members after the meeting
Communication	Minimal team member engagement (e.g. members off-task, distracted)	1 2 3 4 5	High level of engagement from all team members (e.g., verbal input, attention, willingness to complete tasks)
	Discussions disjointed (e.g., numerous interruptions, sidebar conversations)	1 2 3 4 5	Discussions stay on track; no sidebar conversations
	Poor team member communication (e.g., aggressive tones, lack of listening, disrespect)	1 2 3 4 5	Team members communicate effectively (e.g., speak directly, ask questions, express support, restate ideas)
	Disagreements/conflicts aren't addressed (e.g., disgruntled team members, talking behind backs)	1 2 3 4 5	Disagreements/conflicts are addressed (e.g., problem solving, respect, listening)
	Some members are not valued as important to the team	1 2 3 4 5	Members value each other's roles and contributions
	Members are not provided time/forum to share viewpoints; limited discussion time before a decision is made	1 2 3 4 5	All viewpoints shared and given adequate time prior to decision-making (e.g., discussion of options and consequences)
	Final decision made with limited input by team (e.g., one person makes decision, limited influence, no voting)	1 2 3 4 5	Shared decision-making with balanced influence of team members (e.g., voting on decisions, discussion of options)

Tool #6: Team Functioning Scale (cont'd)

Focus	Lack of meeting purpose (e.g., meeting "for the sake of meeting")	1 2 3 4 5	Meeting has clear purpose, which is communicated in advance
	Data does not drive decision-making	1 2 3 4 5	Data drives decision-making (i.e., relevant data is reviewed and discussed; decisions clearly influenced by data)
	No reference to past goals/action items	1 2 3 4 5	Status of action items from last meeting is reviewed
	Action items not identified, unclear responsibilities	1 2 3 4 5	Clear action items (e.g., deadlines, person responsible)
	Meetings are not productive and do not result in progress	1 2 3 4 5	Meetings are productive; continual progress focused on purpose

Note. Reprinted with permission from Team Functioning Scale by A. Gaumer Erickson and P. Noonan. Copyright 2012 by the Center for Research on Learning, University of Kansas.

Tool #7: Action Plan Template

Purpose: This form assists school teams in organizing information on goals and supporting activities, and provides a means for monitoring progress on both.

Team Name:				
Mission Stataement:				
Team Leader(s);		**School District:**		

Goal:				
Steps	**Who**	**By When**	**What is Outcome?**	**Status (Date: Met/ Not met)**

Goal:				
Steps	**Who**	**By When**	**What is Outcome?**	**Status (Date: Met/ Not met)**

Goal:				
Steps	**Who**	**By When**	**What is Outcome?**	**Status (Date: Met/ Not met)**

Tool #8: Shared Leadership Survey

Purpose: This measure helps teams to assess their overall level of shared leadership.

Instructions: Administer the following survey to all group members. Once all members have responded, average their scores by item and by domain to get an idea of the group's sentiment. Consult the key below the blank version in order to see which items fall into each domain.

ITEM	SCORE
(1 = strongly disagree, 3= neutral, 5 = strongly agree)	
I collaborate regularly with my team members to achieve goals.	1 2 3 4 5
My team has a shared vision with agreed-upon goals.	1 2 3 4 5
The formal leaders in my team are willing to delegate some control to informal leaders.	1 2 3 4 5
Our team members trust each other to work effectively and get the job done.	1 2 3 4 5
I understand my team's purpose and goals.	1 2 3 4 5
When major decisions must be made, team members are involved in the decision process in a meaningful way.	1 2 3 4 5
Each team member's unique expertise is valued and utilized.	1 2 3 4 5
When I think of leadership, I think of a shared mission to learn and construct knowledge collaboratively.	1 2 3 4 5
I have an excellent rapport with at least two other team members.	1 2 3 4 5
When a new task arises, leadership responsibilities are determined by members' strengths, not by formal titles.	1 2 3 4 5
I feel confident taking on leadership responsibilities in this team.	1 2 3 4 5
If the team's chairperson left, the team would continue to make progress toward its goals.	1 2 3 4 5
When team members work together as leaders, they share beliefs, values, and goals.	1 2 3 4 5
As a leader in the team, I have responsibilities in multiple roles/positions.	1 2 3 4 5
All members of my team value collective efficacy.	1 2 3 4 5
I know what strengths and skills each of the other team members possesses.	1 2 3 4 5
In addition to the team's formally designated leaders, I can identify at least two other team members who act as informal leaders.	1 2 3 4 5
The leadership roles available in my group result from the needs arising from our goals.	1 2 3 4 5
I feel that every other team member has a capacity for leadership.	1 2 3 4 5
Multiple people are trusted with information and decision making for every activity our group undertakes.	1 2 3 4 5

Tool #8: Shared Leadership Survey (cont'd)

DOMAIN		SCORE
(1 = strongly disagree, 3= neutral, 5 = strongly agree)		
Collaboration	I collaborate regularly with my team members to achieve goals.	1 2 3 4 5
Vision	My team has a shared vision with agreed-upon goals.	1 2 3 4 5
Delegation	The formal leaders in my team are willing to delegate some control to informal leaders.	1 2 3 4 5
Culture	Our team members trust each other to work effectively and get the job done.	1 2 3 4 5
Vision	I understand my team's purpose and goals.	1 2 3 4 5
Delegation	When major decisions must be made, team members are involved in the decision process in a meaningful way.	1 2 3 4 5
Culture	Each team member's unique expertise is valued and utilized.	1 2 3 4 5
Culture	When I think of leadership, I think of a shared mission to learn and construct knowledge collaboratively.	1 2 3 4 5
Collaboration	I have an excellent rapport with at least two other team members.	1 2 3 4 5
Delegation	When a new task arises, leadership responsibilities are determined by members' strengths, not by formal titles.	1 2 3 4 5
Culture	I feel confident taking on leadership responsibilities in this team.	1 2 3 4 5
Delegation	If the team's chairperson left, the team would continue to make progress toward its goals.	1 2 3 4 5
Vision	When team members work together as leaders, they share beliefs, values, and goals.	1 2 3 4 5
Delegation	As a leader in the team, I have responsibilities in multiple roles/positions.	1 2 3 4 5
Culture	All members of my team value collective efficacy.	1 2 3 4 5
Collaboration	I know what strengths and skills each of the other team members possess.	1 2 3 4 5
Collaboration	In addition to the team's formally designated leaders, I can identify at least two other team members who act as informal leaders.	1 2 3 4 5
Vision	The leadership roles available in my group result from the needs arising from our goals.	1 2 3 4 5
Collaboration	I feel that every other team member has a capacity for leadership.	1 2 3 4 5
Delegation	Multiple people are trusted with information and decision making for every activity our group undertakes.	1 2 3 4 5

Note. Reprinted with permission from Shared Leadership Measure by J.A. Brussow. Copyright 2013 by the Center for Research on Learning, University of Kansas.

Tool #9: Sustainability Survey and Sustained Teaming Activities Checklist

Purpose: This survey and checklist can be used to help teams anticipate, discuss, and plan for possible challenges to sustaining their efforts.

Instructions: Have each team member individually complete the following measure. Once all members have completed the scale, aggregate the results to get an idea of your team's overall level of confidence in its future. Then, discuss each question, paying close attention to low-scoring items.

Reflection: Once you have completed the sustainability survey, reflect on low-scoring items to determine the reason for your members' lack of confidence in those areas. Once you have figured out areas to work on for sustainability, consult the following list of activities that promote sustained teaming. Use your identified weaknesses to select the items that you think your team should consider as an activity for a sustainability action plan. Once you have selected 3-5 items, discuss the possibility of including each one in your action plan.

ITEM	RATING
(1 = not confident at all, 5 = most confident)	
How confident are you that your team will achieve your team goals?	5 4 3 2 1
Why?	
How confident are you that your team will share responsibility in implementing activities?	5 4 3 2 1
Why or why not?	
How confident are you that the community transition team will produce lasting benefits for each team member's agency?	5 4 3 2 1
Why?	5 4 3 2 1
How confident are you that your community transition team will be around for 1 year?	5 4 3 2 1
Why?	
How confident are you that your community transition team will be around for 5 years?	5 4 3 2 1
Why?	

Tool #9: Sustainability Survey and Sustained Teaming Activities Checklist (cont'd)

	Ensure team members view team activities as effective and meaningful
	Communicate and delegate duties to engage members
	Make sure leadership effectively promotes and supports collaboration
	Provide for ongoing evaluation or monitoring of success
	Use public relations to improve visibility and secure community support
	Use outreach activities to promote political support from district and state levels
	Present to the school board or Chamber of Commerce
	Plan a transition fair to connect resources to students and families
	Build upon established activities
	Create projects that also help partner organizations
	Expand network of resources by recruiting new stakeholders/prospective members
	Create a list of community resources: services/organizations/businesses
	Invite presenters to meetings
	Give awards/recognition to key individuals and organizations to encourage participation
	Provide continual, high-quality professional development and/or assistance for team members
	Integrate teaming structures into daily lives of the school community
	Develop mission, vision, and/or case for support
	Develop bylaws
	Establish a web site
	Develop letter of introduction
	Create a logo
	Create a quarterly newsletter
	Set up press release detailing activities or upcoming events to various newspapers
	Outline proposed yearly activities to determine amount of funding needed for sustainability
	Research and identify potential sources of funding
	Apply for funding

Note. Reprinted with permission from Sustainability Survey and Sustained Teaming Activities Checklist by J. Soukup. Copyright 2008 by the Center for Research on Learning, University of Kansas.

Tool #10: Sample Bylaws

Sample Bylaws

ARTICLE I—NAME AND PURPOSE

The Sample Community Transition Team (SCTT) was formed as a means to gather community leaders to assist students in achieving success in life experiences beyond their secondary educational careers by collaborating to develop resources to be utilized by students and families. The SCTT will seek the involvement of a wide variety of organizations and individuals from the county area who have knowledge and resources related to our mission and values.

ARTICLE II—MEMBERSHIP

Anyone who has an interest in and can make a contribution to the mission of SCTT is welcome to join. No special requirements or skills are needed other than the desire to help high school students achieve success. Interested individuals may express interest in joining by contacting any member of the SCTT; SCTT members will in turn notify the president of the SCTT, who will bring the recommendation to the full SCTT for acceptance.

To be in good standing with the team, individuals must attend 50% of regular meetings and 75% of their assigned committee meetings in a calendar year. Attendance will be taken at all meetings to determine good standing. Lack of attendance or participation may be cause for removal from the SCTT.

Non-members will not be allowed to vote on issues brought before the SCTT or serve on committees.

ARTICLE III—ORGANIZATIONAL STRUCTURE

The duties of the president of the SCTT are to conduct and preside over all meetings, prepare the agenda and notify members of meetings, contact members if meetings are cancelled, and facilitate the formation of any new committees.

The vice president of the SCTT will conduct meetings in the absence of the President and assist the president as requested; the vice president will succeed to the presidency after serving as vice president.

The secretary of the SCTT will take minutes for all regular meetings and will maintain other correspondence such as committee reports, press releases, and so on. The treasurer of the SCTT will maintain all financial accounts for the SCTT and give a financial report at each regular meeting..

Officer Election

Nominations will be taken from the floor at the May meeting, with voting being held at the same meeting. The term of office will be for 1 year. Officers must be in good standing to remain in office. A special election will be held when there is a vacant position.

Tool #10: Sample Bylaws (cont'd)

Voting Procedure

A quorum will constitute 51% of the members in good standing. For the first year of the SCTT, good standing will be defined as not missing more than two consecutive meetings (including both regular and committee meetings). After the first year, good standing will be defined as 50% attendance at regular meetings and 75% attendance at committee meetings for a calendar year.

Voting will take place by the raising of hands and hands will be counted by the president or an individual acting in place of the president. If more than one nomination is made for a given office, paper ballots will be provided and the president and secretary will tally the results.

ARTICLE IV—MEETINGS

The regular meetings of the SCTT will occur quarterly; committee meetings will be held as needed. Regular meetings will be held on the third Thursday of the month beginning at 3:30 pm. In the event of conflicting schedule (e.g., holidays) the SCTT may choose an alternate date. The president or vice president will notify members by e-mail of any change to the time or date of a regular meeting or if there is a need for a special meeting. Members who cannot attend a meeting should notify the president or the committee chair. Members will participate in organization events and serve on committees. For a regular SCTT meeting to be official, either the president or the vice president must be in attendance. For the SCTT to conduct business there must be a quorum (51% of members in good standing).

When voting, a simple majority of the members in good standing will determine whether a motion passes or fails. The president of the SCTT will be a non-voting member unless there is a tie. If there is a tie, the President's vote will be the tie breaker. The president will facilitate all regular meetings and the secretary will take the minutes. Robert's Rules of Order will be used.

ARTICLE V—COMMITTEES

The standing committees for the SCTT include Transition Fair, Fundraising, Marketing, and Bylaws. Although membership in each committee will be on a volunteer basis, the president has the right to assign members and appoint committee chairs. Chairs will notify committee members of committee meetings and assign a member to take notes at each committee meeting.

ARTICLE VI—AMENDMENTS

Membership must vote on any changes to the bylaws. Members in good standing will vote on changes as needed. Any member in good standing can propose changes. Changes may be voted on at any time. Unless otherwise stipulated, a quorum (51% of members in good standing) is required to pass any changes to the bylaws.

References

Asselin, S. B., Todd-Allen, M., & deFur, S. (1998). Transition coordinators. *TEACHING Exceptional Children, 30*, 11–15.

Benitez, D. T., Morningstar, M. E., & Frey, B. B. (2009). A multistate survey of special education teachers' perceptions of their transition competencies. *Career Development and Transition for Exceptional Individuals, 32*(1), 6–16. http://dx.doi.org/10.1177/0885728808323945

Benz, M. R., Johnson, D. K., Mikkelsen, K. S., & Lindstrom, L. E. (1995). Improving collaboration between schools and vocational rehabilitation: Stakeholder identified barriers and strategies. *Career Development for Exceptional Individuals, 18*(2), 133–144. http://dx.doi.org/10.1177/088572889501800207

Bishop, K. K., Wolf, J., & Arango, P. (1993). *Family/professional collaboration for children with special health care needs and their families.* Burlington, VT: Department of Social Work, University of Vermont.

Blalock, G. (1996). Community transition teams as the foundation for transition services for youth with learning disabilities. *Journal of Learning Disabilities, 29*, 148–159. http://dx.doi.org/10.1177/002221949602900204

Blalock, G., & Benz, M. R. (1999). *Using community transition teams to improve transition services.* Austin, TX: PRO-ED.

Brussow, J. A. (2013). *Shared leadership measure.* Lawrence, KS: University of Kansas Center for Research on Learning.

Carter, E., Owen, L., Sweden, B., Trainor, A, Thompson, C., Ditchman, N., & Cole, O., (2009). Conversations that matter: Engaging communities to expand employment opportunities for youth with disabilities. *TEACHING Exceptional Children, 41*(6), 38–46.

Cashman, J. (1995). Collaboration and reform: The role of interagency linkages in developing a coherent strategy for transition. *Journal for Vocational Special Needs Education, 17*, 103–107.

Clark, G., & McDonnell, J. (1994). The role of local transition councils in rural communities. *Rural Special Education Quarterly, 13*(1), 3–8.

Cozzens, G., Dowdy, C. A., & Smith, T. E. C. (1999). *Adult agencies: Linkages for adolescents in transition.* Austin, TX: PRO-ED.

Crane, K., & Mooney, M. (2005). *Essential tools: Community resource mapping.* Minneapolis, MN: University of Minnesota, Institute on Community Integration, National Center on Secondary Education and Transition. Retrieved from http://www.ncset.org/publications/essentialtools/mapping/

deFur, S. H. (1997). Collaboration as a prevention tool for youth with disabilities. *Preventing School Failure, 41,* 173–178. http://dx.doi.org/10.1080/10459889709603289

deFur, S. H., & Taymans, J. M. (1995). Competencies needed for transition specialists in vocational rehabilitation, vocational education, and special education. *Exceptional Children, 62,* 38–52.

Division on Career Development and Transition. (2000, March). *Transition specialist competencies* [Fact sheet]. Arlington, VA: Council for Exceptional Children. Retrieved from http://www.nsttac.org/sites/default/files/assets/pdf/DCDTFactSheeCompentencies.pdf

Dunst, C. J., & Bruder, M. B. (2002). Valued outcomes of service coordination, early intervention, and natural environments. *Exceptional Children, 68,* 361–375.

Feldman, J., & Tung, R. (2001, April). *Whole school reform: How schools use the data-based inquiry and decision making process.* Paper presented at the 82nd annual meeting of the American Educational Research Association, Seattle, WA.

Ferber, T., Pittman, K., & Marshall, T. (2002). *State youth policy: Helping all youth to grow up fully prepared and fully engaged.* Takoma Park, MD: The Forum for Youth Investment, 2002.

Florian, J. (2000). *Sustaining education reform: Influential factors* (Report No. EA 031023). Aurora, CO: Mid Continent Research for Education and Learning. (ERIC Document Reproduction Service No. ED 453 583).

Freudenberg, N., & Ruglis, J. (2007). Reframing school dropout as a public health issue. *Preventing Chronic Disease: Public Health Research, Practice, and Policy, 4*(4), 1–11. Retrieved from http://www.ncbi.nlm.nih.gov/pmc/articles/PMC2099272/pdf/PCD44A107.pdf

Frey, B. B., Lohmeier, J. H., Lee, S. W., Tollefson, N., & Johanning, M. L. (2006). Measuring collaboration among grant partners. *American Journal of Evaluation, 27,* 383-392. http://dx.doi.org/10.1177/1098214006290356

Gajda, R. (2004). Utilizing collaboration theory to evaluate strategic alliances. *American Journal of Evaluation, 25,* 65–77.

Gaumer Erickson, A. (2012). *Transition assessment framework.* Lawrence, KS: University of Kansas Center for Research on Learning.

Gaumer Erickson, A., & Noonan, P. (2012). *Team functioning scale.* Lawrence, KS: University of Kansas Center for Research on Learning.

Gaumer Erickson, A., & Noonan, P. (2013). *Indicators of college and career readiness survey.* Lawrence, KS: University of Kansas Center for Research on Learning.

Golden, N., & Gall, J. P. (2000). *The complete toolkit for building high-performance work teams.* Eugene, OR: University of Oregon ERIC Clearinghouse on Educational Management. Retrieved from https://scholarsbank.uoregon.edu/xmlui/bitstream/handle/1794/3295/toolkit.pdf?sequence=1

Gronn, P. (2000). Distributed properties: A new architecture for leadership. *Educational Management and Administration, 28*, 317–338. http://dx.doi.org/10.1177/0263211X000283006

Hair, E., Ling, T., & Cochran, S. W. (2003). *Youth development programs and educationally disadvantaged older youths: A synthesis.* Washington, DC: Child Trends. Retrieved from http://www.childtrends.org/files/EducDisadvOlderYouth.pdf

Harris, A. (2003). Teacher leadership as distributed leadership: Heresy, fantasy or possibility? *School Leadership & Management, 23*, 313–324. http://dx.doi.org/10.1080/1363243032000112801

Hasazi, S., Furney, K., DeStefano, L., & Johnson, D. (1999, April 20). *State and local education efforts to implement the transition requirements of the Individuals with Disabilities Education Act (IDEA): Report on the national survey of the implementation of the IDEA transition requirements.* Burlington, VT: University of Vermont.

Hogue, T. (1993). *Community-based collaboration: Community wellness multiplied.* Bend, OR: Chandler Center for Community Leadership. Retrieved from http://crs.uvm.edu/nnco/collab/wellness.html

IDEA regulations, 34 C.F.R. § 300 (2012).

Individuals With Disabilities Education Act, 20 U.S.C. §§ 1400 *et seq.* (2006 & Supp. V. 2011).

Jenson, R. (2012). *Agenda template for the Missouri SPDG project management team.* Kansas City, MO: University of Missouri Institute for Human Development.

Johnson, D. R., Thurlow, M. L., & Stout, K. E. (2007). *Revisiting graduation requirements and diploma options for youth with disabilities: A national study* (Technical Report 49). Minneapolis, MN: University of Minnesota, National Center on Educational Outcomes.

Johnson, L. J., Zorn, D., Tam, B. K., Lamontagne, M., & Johnson, S. A. (2003). Stakeholders' views of factors that impact successful interagency collaboration. *Exceptional Children, 69*, 195–209.

Kansas Department of Labor. (2013). *Labor market information services.* Retrieved from http://www.dol.ks.gov/LMIS/Default.aspx

Kleinhammer-Tramill, P. J., & Rosenkoetter, S. E. (1994). Early intervention and secondary/transition services: Harbingers of change in education. *Focus on Exceptional Children, 27*(2), 1–14.

Lambert, L. (2002). A framework for shared leadership. *Beyond Instructional Leadership, 59*(8), 37–40.

Landsberger, J. (2012). *Cooperative learning series: Active listening.* Retrieved from http://www.studygs.net/listening.htm

Mattessich, P. (2003). *Can this collaboration be saved? Twenty factors that can make or break any group effort.* Montclair, NJ: National Housing Institute. Retrieved from http://www.nhi.org

Mattessich, P., & Monsey, B. (1992). *Collaboration: What makes it work. A review of research literature on factors influencing successful collaboration.* St, Paul, MN: Amherst H. Wilder Foundation.

Morningstar, M., Noonan, P., & Soukup, J. (2010). *Arizona community transition teams training manual.* Lawrence: University of Kansas Center for Research on Learning.

Morningstar, M. E., Kleinhammer-Tramill, P. J., & Lattin, D. L. (1999). Using successful models of student-centered transition planning and services for adolescents with disabilities. *Focus on Exceptional Children, 31*(9), 2–20.

National High School Center. (2007, May). *State and district-level support for successful transitions into high school. Policy brief.* Washington, DC: Author. Retrieved from http://www.betterhighschools.org/docs/NHSC_PolicyBrief_TransitionsIntoHighSchool.pdf

Newman, L., Wagner, M., Cameto, R., Knokey, A. M., & Shaver, D. (2010). *Comparisons across time of the outcomes of youth with disabilities up to 4 years after high school: A report of findings from the national longitudinal transition study (NLTS) and the national longitudinal transition study-2 (NLTS2).* Menlo Park, CA: SRI International.

Noonan, P. (2011). *Community transition team process checklist.* Lawrence: University of Kansas Center for Research on Learning.

Noonan, P., Gaumer Erickson, A., & Morningstar, M. (2012). *Transition collaboration survey.* Lawrence: University of Kansas Center for Research on Learning.

Noonan, P., Gaumer Erickson, A., & Morningstar, M. (2013). Effects of community transition teams on interagency collaboration for school and adult agency staff. *Career Development for Exceptional Individuals, 36*, on p.8, 9, 96-104. http://dx.doi.org/10.1177/2165143412451119

Noonan, P. M., & Morningstar, M. E. (2012). Effective strategies for interagency collaboration. In M. L. Wehmeyer & K. W. Webb (Eds.), *Handbook of adolescent transition education for youth with disabilities* (pp. 312–328). New York, NY: Routledge.

Noonan, P. M., Morningstar, M. E., & Gaumer Erickson, A. (2008). Improving interagency collaboration: Effective strategies used by high-performing local districts and communities. *Career Development for Exceptional Individuals, 31*, 132–143. http://dx.doi.org/10.1177/0885728808327149

Noyes, D. A., & Sax, C. L. (2004). Changing systems for transition: Students, families, and professionals working together. *Education and Training in Developmental Disabilities, 39*(1), 35–44.

PACER Center, n.d. *Interagency collaboration and transition.* http://www.pacer.org/tatra/resources/inter.asp

Peterson, N. L. (1991). Interagency collaboration under Part H: The key to comprehensive, multidisciplinary, coordinated infant/toddler intervention services. *Journal of Early Intervention, 15*, 89–105. http://dx.doi.org/10.1177/105381519101500111

Poff, J., & Parks, D. (2010). Is shared leadership right for your school district? *Journal of Scholarship and Practice, 6*(4), 29–39.

Robinson, S. (2013, March 13). Career exploration class helps students find employment. *Democrat News.* Retrieved from http://dailyjournalonline.com/democrat-news/news/local/school-news/career-exploration-class-helps-students-find-employment/article_97475052-8c09-11e2-aae4-0019bb2963f4.html

Skalski, A. K., & Romero, M. (2011). Data-based decision making. *Principal Leadership, 11*(5), 12–16. Retrieved from http://www.nasponline.org/resources/principals/Data_Use_Jan11_NASSP.PDF

Soukup, J. (2008). *Sustainability survey and sustained teaming activities checklist.* Lawrence, KS: University of Kansas Center for Research on Learning.

Special School District of St. Louis County. *Resource directory. Transition related services for persons with disabilities in the greater St. Louis area.* (2012). St. Louis, MO: Author. Rertrieved from http://www.ssdmo.org/assets/123/step3/Resource_Directory.pdf

Spillane, J. P., & Healey, K. (2010). Conceptualizing school leadership and management from a distributed perspective: An exploration of some study options and measures. *The Elementary School Journal, 111*, 253–281. http://dx.doi.org/10.1086/656300

Stodden, R. A., Brown, S.E., Galloway, L. M., Mrazek, S., & Noy, L. (2005). *Essential tools: Interagency transition team development and facilitation.* Minneapolis, MN: National Center on Secondary Education and Transition. Retrieved from http://www.ncset.org/publications/essentialtools/teams/EssentialTools_Teams.pdf

Stringfield, S., Wayman, J. C., & Yakimowski, M. (2005). Scaling up data use in classrooms, schools and districts. In C. Dede, J. P. Honan, & L. C. Peters (Eds.), *Scaling up success: Lessons learned from technology-based educational innovation* (pp. 133–152). San Francisco, CA: Jossey-Bass.

Swanson, C. B. (2009). *Closing the graduation gap: Educational and economic conditions in America's largest cities.* Bethesda, MD: Editorial Projects in Education.

Taylor, H., Krane, D., & Orkis, K. (2010). *The ADA, 20 years later.* New York, NY: Harris Interactive. Retrieved from http://www.2010disabilitysurveys.org/pdfs/surveyresults.pdf

Timmons, J. C., Cohen, A., & Fesko, S. L. (2004). Merging cultural differences and professional identities: Strategies for maximizing collaborative efforts during the implementation of the Workforce Investment Act. *Journal of Rehabilitation, 70*, 19–27.

Timperley, H. (2005). Distributed leadership: Developing theory from practice. *Journal of Curriculum Studies, 37*, 395–420. http://dx.doi.org/10.1080/00220270500038545